WOUNDED HEART,
HEALED HEART

WOUNDED HEART, HEALED HEART

Robert Lindenberger

Pleasant W rd

Endorsements

Pain. It's a fact of life. We do what we can to avoid pain, either emotional or physical, yet pain is an unavoidable part of life that shapes and molds our character, either for bad or for good.

In his first book, *Wounded Heart, Healed Heart,* Author Robert Lindenberger takes an honest and revealing look at pain and endeavors to put it into perspective, to give us insight on transforming those awful scars into something helpful, perhaps even beautiful, as we yield them to God.

If you're struggling, unable to overcome the hurts of the past, this book can't help but be a valuable and timely aid in the recovery process.

—Nancy Arant Williams, Author and Speaker

All of us are wounded at some times in our lives. It may be by a close friend or a relative or through adverse circumstances. The hurt can be deep and long lasting if we suppress it. Jesus came to set us free from our wounds and give us a new life. One of the ways Jesus can set us free is through the advice and counsel of others who have gone through similar hurts or experiences.

In *Wounded Heart, Healed Heart* Robert Lindenberger provides us with a vehicle of healing that is based on his own life experience and how Jesus can make the final difference. For those who have undergone similar circumstances, this book will help them to see Jesus in a new way—a way that will help to free them from the bondage of negativity and release them into the positive world of the kingdom of God here on earth.

—James Sohaney, Christian Author and Speaker.
President of a small power development company.

Many individuals write books that chronicle painful situations, but Robert Lindenberger is not satisfied with dolling out paragraph upon paragraph testifying to what he's endured. In *Wounded Heart, Healed Heart* every page overflows with words that bring understanding and tranquility to the suffering soul. Here is a man who has undergone the worst and returns, not retribution, but peace. Mr. Lindenberger is a courageous man who bares his soul in order to lift others to the throne where grace will set them free.

—Louise Bergmann DuMont, Author and Speaker.
www.louisedumont.com

No dry, academic study, this – Robert Lindenberger's gift is to carry us with him, step for step and tear for tear, through dark and painful times to where God can use our hurts to heal others.

—Glenn Killinger

Doloias

May God bless you real good. Keep
on keeping on serving Jesus.

God bless

Robert Buckley

Pleasant Word (a division of WinePress Publishing, PO Box 428, Enumclaw, WA 98022) functions only as book publisher. As such, the ultimate design, content, editorial accuracy, and views expressed or implied in this work are those of the author.

Some Scriptures are taken from the Holy Bible, New International Version, Copyright © 1973, 1978, 1980 by the International Bible Society. Used by permission of Zondervan All rights reserved.

Some Scriptures are taken from the Holy Bible, King James Version of the Bible.

ISBN 13: 978-1-4141-0915-2
ISBN 10: 1-4141-0915-6
Library of Congress Catalog Card Number: 2006910528

Dedication

In memory of Gennaro Marchese, whom I grew to love over the four years I spent as his privileged caretaker, adopted, as I was by his dear, godly family. It is because of them that this book has become a possibility.

Poppa Marchese graduated to glory on December 16, 2004 at the age of ninety-one, but he will live on in my heart—beloved and never forgotten.

Table of Contents

Foreword

We have all encountered the awkward presence of people who have seeping emotional or spiritual wounds in their lives. They are often dominated by anger, fear, or any number of reflex reactions that shape their view of the world around them. The lingering hurt and pain from the past interprets all they experience today. They often carry within the inner chamber of their heart and mind secrets that pester them with resounding accusations of belittlement and failure. Vicious echoes from the past.

Yesterday's victim can easily become today's perpetrator. Those who have been abused can become the abuser, the sexually violated can become the violators; it graduates from an experience to a chain reaction. "Wounded people wound people" is more than a catchy phrase. It, too, often is reality.

Robert Lindenberger has removed the cover off his own inner struggles. He writes to us not from the vantage point of a therapeutic expert, but a wounded healer. He points the way not as the distant practitioner but as a fellow traveler. His goal is obvious; to provide sources of identification and helpful direction.

As I read through this manuscript, I realized this is not for everyone. It is an invitation for those who have felt the excruciating pain of life's wounds to enter into a dialogue with someone else who has walked the same path. There he not only seeks to disclose his wounded heart, but to unlock his source of healing.

My prayer is that your journey may lead you to personal enlightenment and lasting healing.

Harry F. Wood, ThD, District Superintendent of Penn-Jersey District of the Wesleyan Church.

Introduction

It has been said that the Church of Jesus Christ is the only army that shoots its wounded.

I would argue that every human being who lives long enough experiences pain of one kind or another, but it's unfortunate that it happens in the body of Christ.

Occasionally, the person responsible for the blow has no idea what he has done, but sometimes the injury is purposeful, causing no end of pain, perhaps not physical, but even worse, leaving permanent emotional scars.

This book has taken over 50 years to put together. I have experienced a wounded spirit, but most important, I am experiencing a healed spirit by my friend and Savior Jesus Christ. It is my hope that this book will bring healing and hope as you journey with me through an examination of emotional pain.

Prologue

He was a handsome man, huge and physically imposing. Hercules? Whoever he was, he was clearly a survivor. In fact, he had just lost his wife and infant in childbirth, and only dogged determination kept him living alone in the wilderness.

One night after a long day in the fields, he ate the last of the sourdough bread and finished the goats' milk, planning to turn in early.

Suddenly, a deafening commotion exploded on his senses, coming from the direction of the barn. Only partially dressed, he grabbed his gun off the wall and ran toward the racket.

It was already too late. The barn door hung on one hinge, and there in the straw lay his milk goat, mauled and mutilated by a grizzly.

As hate seized him, he purposed in his heart to hunt down that bear or die trying.

Early the next morning, he rose, planning his revenge. He rolled his clothes and provisions into a pack and gathered enough food to last for a while, then stuffed his pockets with shotgun shells and followed the blood trail. The overgrown path led through an increasingly dense thicket of trees and brush, but he pushed on, driven by hate, until he saw a clearing just ahead. He knew by the smell that the bear was nearby, but stepped back in shock and horror when suddenly the behemoth confronted him, let out an earth-shaking roar and lunged.

With one swipe of his huge paw, claws slashed through soft flesh, and the man, now badly injured, lost his footing and rolled down an embankment into a stream, where he lay, partially submerged. The bear, now satisfied, dropped on all fours, shook his head from side to side, and ambled off.

When the man finally regained consciousness, it took every ounce of strength to crawl from the quickly rising water. After taking stock of his wounds, he knew he would never be the same again. One arm, out of joint, hung lifeless at his side, while the other was covered by slash marks and blood. His right leg could bear weight, but the left had an open, compound fracture. With only one eye remaining, he lay there for a long time before forcing himself to move, and finally crawled to where his pack had fallen. After cleaning his wounds as best he could, he ate and rested, then painstakingly fashioned a crutch from a tree branch, and slowly, agonizingly, made his way toward home.

Can you identify with his pain?

Part I

CHAPTER ONE

Types of Pain

SELF-INFLICTED PAIN

Picture in your mind if you will: the setting is an Old West town, the saloon looming large on the wide main Street. In front is a narrow wooden hitching post, where an old donkey is tied, and on the board sidewalk, a man sits in a chair propped back against the weathered clapboard building, with his hat pulled down to shade his eyes from the glare of the sun.

A swaggering kid, wearing a brand new gun belt around his skinny waist, is out to make his mark on the world. Standing in front of the donkey now, he punches it in the head with all his might, the donkey brays in pain, and shortly falls to its knees.

The boy laughs in glee, thrilled to have wielded such power.

Outside the saloon, the man, now sitting up in his chair, leans forward and cocks his hat to get a better look at the cocky kid.

"Why did you do that?"

The kid shrugs his shoulders, smirking confidently. "Cause I wanted to."

The old man tilts his head, glaring at the boy. "Don't that old mule have feelings?"

"Don't much care if he does or don't."

After a moment's pause, the old man cocks his hat once again. "Nice gun you got there. New?"

"Yep. And I know how to use it, too."

"Well now. Let's see if you got feelings. Put your hand on the gun in the holster."

The old man speaks with such authority that the boy, without thinking, obeys.

"Now, pull the trigger."

Aghast, the boy frowns. "No. I'll shoot myself in the foot."

"Yep. That's just what you're going to do. Now you pull that trigger, or I'll shoot you in the knee."

With no other choice, the boy does as he's told and lets out an ear-piercing scream.

Standing to his feet, the old man, looking serious, regards the embarrassed, weeping boy. "Now, maybe you know how the mule felt. Get yourself over to doc's, and if you're lucky, that thing will heal by the time you grow up." After a pause, he added, "Oh, and one more thing. When people ask you what happened, you tell them you shot yourself in the foot."

The boy turned away, having learned a lesson he would never forget–that he had ultimately caused his own pain by his callous disregard for the feelings of the donkey. From now on, he would think before hurting another, man or beast.

Self-inflicted wounds occur when we, as carnal Christians, take it upon ourselves to wield power that belongs only to a sovereign and loving God. The pain comes with facing the consequences of our own sinful behavior. It can be healed, however, if we run to the cross and repent. That wound only becomes chronic if we refuse to face our sin and ask forgiveness, building a wall of self-protection that isolates us from both God and our own guilty conscience. The result is a heart that is calloused and cold, one that cannot be easily touched or broken. When we, instead of God, assume the position of power in our lives, thinking only of what we want, we can speak before we think, easily injuring others.

It is also possible to suffer a wounded spirit because of a wrong concept of God.

EXTERNALLY-INFLICTED PAIN

Sometimes someone else inflicts the wound– as if by a pistol, held in the hand of another. Some wounds are fatal and some are not. Even after the wound heals, the pain remains, and a scar is an ever-present reminder of the incident. Think about the worst physical pain you've ever experienced. Perhaps you can identify with the pain of the man mauled by the bear.

I'd like you to consider this question. Do you have a wounded spirit? Maybe you're asking–What is a wounded spirit?

A wounded spirit occurs when a respected friend or loved one in some way denigrates our value as a person, leaving us feeling defensive and vulnerable.

Let's examine some scriptures that discuss this issue.

Proverbs 18:4 makes a statement and then asks a vital question: *The spirit of a man will sustain infirmity* (sickness, disease, weakness), *but a wounded spirit who can bear?* (KJV)

A man may be able to endure difficult physical wounds, like the man mauled by the bear, but when a person's spirit is wounded, it affects the way he deals with all aspects of his life, breaking down his ability to cope with, and rise above, trials.

Proverbs 15:13–*A merry heart maketh a cheerful countenance, but by sorrow of the heart the spirit is broken.* (KJV)

Proverbs 17:22–*A merry heart does good like a medicine: but a broken heart will dry the bones.* (KJV)

Hebrews 12:15–*Looking diligently lest any man fail of the grace of God; lest any root of bitterness springing up trouble you, and thereby many be defiled.* (KJV)

Ephesians 4:22-24–*That ye put off concerning the former conversation the old man, which is correct according to the deceitful lusts; and be renewed in the spirit of your mind; and that ye put on the new man, which after God is created in righteousness and true holiness.* (KJV)

Following are scriptures that show how the wounded spirit is manifested.

Ezekiel 36:26–*A new heart also will I give you, and a new spirit I will put within you; and I will take away the stony heart out of your flesh, and I will give you an heart of flesh.* (KJV)

Psalm 95:8-11 puts it another way. *Harden not your heart, as in the provocation, as in the day of temptation in the wilderness: When your fathers tempted me, proved me and saw my work. Forty years long was I grieved with this generation, and said, It is a people that do err in their hearts, and they have not known my ways; unto whom I swear in my wrath that they should not enter into my rest.* (KJV)

Another manifestation of a wounded spirit is a slumbering heart. Those with this condition come to God verbally, giving assent with their minds, but never develop a real heart relationship with Him. This relationship lacks the intimacy God yearned for at the creation.

Romans 11:8-10–*According as it is written, God has given them the spirit of slumber, eyes that they should not see, and ears that they should not hear; unto this day. And David saith, Let their table be made a snare, and a trap, and a stumbling block and a recompense unto them: Let their eyes be darkened, that they may not see, and bow down their back always.* (KJV)

Romans 13:11–*And that knowing the time, that now is high time to awake out of sleep; for now is our salvation nearer than when we believed.* (KJV)

I am living proof of God's ability to restore someone from a deep spiritual sleep. By giving me a new revelation of Himself, He put in me a yearning for intimacy, that deep desire to be both fully known and deeply loved.

Those wounded in spirit can also experience what is called an *imprisoned spirit*, from which one cannot escape, manifesting in depression and a sense of bitter despair, leading to hopelessness. This believer sees no hope for a better future, in spite of knowing the promises of God.

Psalm 28:1–*Unto thee I will cry, O Lord my rock; be not silent to me, lest if thou be silent to me, I become like them that go down into the pit.* (KJV)

Isaiah 42:22–*But this is a people robbed and spoiled; they are all of them snared in holes, and they are hid in prison house: they are for a prey, and none delivereth; for a spoil, and none saith, Restore.* (KJV)

Psalm 88: 4-10–*I am counted with them that go down into the pit; I am as a man that has no strength; Free among the dead, like the slain that lie in the grave, whom thou rememberest no more: and they are cut off from thy hand. Thou hast laid me in the lowest pit, in darkness, in the deeps. Thy wrath lieth hard upon me, and thou hast afflicted me in all thy waves. Thou hast put away mine acquaintance from me; thou hast made me an abomination unto them: I am shut up, and I cannot come forth. Mine eyes mourneth by reason of affliction: Lord, I have called daily upon thee, I have stretched out my hands unto thee. Wilt thou show wonders to the dead? Shall the dead arise and praise thee?* (KJV)

The church and those who are in it can sometimes condemn to helplessness and despair one with a wounded spirit. But this is not the way Jesus intended His church to be. Rather, He envisioned His church, His bride, yielded to the Spirit as gentle, encouraging and kind to those who need to see Jesus with skin on. And if the church functions as He intended, it will bring healing and wholeness to those who are hurting.

DOWN BUT NOT OUT

Do you find it difficult to relate to others or to fit into the world around you? Are you finding it hard to cope? You may have a wounded spirit. The heart (or the spirit) is the source of life. It is the center of our being. If the spirit is damaged or wounded (and the Bible says it can be), our ability to relate normally to others, to ourselves, and to God is hampered. *Keep and guard your heart with all vigilance and above all that you guard (your heart), for out of it flows the springs of life (Proverbs 4:23).*

Damage to the human spirit occurs in varying degrees.

For a small minority of the wounded, the damage is only slight, and these people are able to get on with their lives, with only a minimum of irritation or inconvenience. This is what I call a flesh wound. The bullet goes in and through, but does not hit the bone or an internal organ. The wound is sore, but heals quickly with no lasting complications.

Many of the wounded are more deeply affected, going through life with a visible limp. These people can lead relatively normal lives, but may fail to realize their full potential in friendships, marriage, or in relationships with others. These are the ones who sustained damage to not only the flesh but also the bone. The bone heals, but a scar remains, and its victim goes through life with a constant reminder of the injury.

Then there is the person with severe damage to his spirit. He is greatly incapacitated—dysfunctional—with all manner of emotional, psychological, physical and even social disabilities. He may need to be (emotionally) carried through life.

The prophet Jeremiah lived during the Babylonian invasions around 627 B.C., about 100 years after Isaiah's prophesies. Jeremiah was born into a priestly family at Anathoth, a few miles north of Jerusalem. God called him at an early age and showed him snapshots of what would come next. In Jeremiah 23:9, he says, *my heart is broken within me.* He says this because he sees himself suffering from injuries inflicted by pastors, shepherds and prophets, who have failed in their leadership responsibilities.

Broken hearts and wounded spirits can result from the actions of our families, friends and close acquaintances. Let's explore how some of these occur.

GUILT

Let me begin by making this statement. An unmistakable connection can be made between unresolved guilt and the likelihood of developing physical and spiritual illness, and even death. *My guilt has overwhelmed me like a burden too heavy to bear. My words fester…I am bowed down and brought very low…there is no health in my body…even the light has gone from my eyes (Psalm 38:4-10).*

I told a dear brother in Christ that I was writing a book on the subject of a wounded spirit and he shared this story. Let me set the stage. My friend is a few years younger, but a whole lot brighter, than I. We attended Bible School together at the time when psychology was just coming into its own. The psychologists of the day suggested strongly that only they, and not pastors, were capable of dealing with emotional problems. After all, pastors were only preachers and not counselors. Keep in mind that this occurred at the time Viet Nam veterans were returning home to rejection and public derision.

A returning Viet Nam veteran went to my pastor friend for counseling. After hearing his story, my sensitive friend realized this gentleman was suffering from post-traumatic stress disorder and referred him to a so-called Christian psychologist. The struggling man saw the Christian psychologist, only to hear that his struggles had occurred because he needed to get right with God. The injured man was already a born-again Christian, so this pronouncement caused untold guilt and feelings of hopelessness. With nowhere else to turn, he used his service revolver to commit suicide.

My friend is a wise and educated man, but continues to suffer from the pain of that man's death. He has overcome, to some extent, that wound, but the ache that remains will never let him forget the incident. My friend's restored equilibrium has come only after applying the ointment of scripture that says, *There is now no condemnation to those who are in Christ Jesus* (Romans 8:1). And *If we confess our sin, He (Jesus Christ) is faithful and just to forgive us our sins, and cleanse us from all unrighteousness* (1 John 1:9).

But this scenario could have gone in another direction. If my friend had not overcome the guilt and pain caused by this man's death, he might have left the ministry altogether. And in that case, countless numbers of pastors and other hurting people would have gone without his help.

Guilt is much like the pain experienced from accidentally touching a flame. The pain warns us to move quickly, before serious injury occurs. Yet that same guilt, in the form of Holy Spirit conviction, can also have positive results, by stirring the conscience to see and admit failure and to point us to the cross, where we can receive forgiveness and cleansing. If guilt is not resolved, it can fester deep inside, causing anguish and even physical suffering.

In his book, *Hope for the Troubled Heart,* Billy Graham says,

Responses to grief are as varied as grief itself. While some people want to die, others blow up. They shout and curse the world and blaspheme God. Sociologists have tried to grade the types of grief according to their severity, but no one can put a magnifying glass on another's hurts, except God.

Many times grief is accompanied by guilt; whether real or false, guilt compounds grief. With false guilt, we fall into the trap of "if onlys." "If only we had been home, we might have been able to get the paramedics in time." "If only we hadn't said she could stay out until midnight." These thoughts are normal emotions when we feel guilty about something over which we have no control.

Then there is real guilt. Emotions become raw when we know we have disobeyed man's or God's laws or have become careless with what God has given us."[1].

Mr. Graham goes on with an illustration about a man driving down the street, while his wife holds their six-month old baby in her lap. The man turns the corner and has a head-on collision, and the baby dies on impact. The man is charged with manslaughter for not having the baby in the proper car seat. Mr. Graham concludes by saying, "Imagine the amount of grief compounded by guilt in that poor father's heart."[2]

Unkind Words

"Why are you in the house on such a beautiful day? You should be outside playing with your friends." Her mother hit a raw nerve and Girta began to cry.

"What's wrong, honey? Why are you so sad?"

"I don't want to talk about it," cried Girta.

Her mother called Girta her baby even though she was almost seven. She pulled her close to her breast and cuddled her as she spoke softly, "My baby. Mmm, mmmm, Mommy's here. Let mommy make it all better."

Girta pulled away, stopped crying, and looked at her mother as she said, "They call me names and I don't like it. They call me dirty Jew."

Her mother grabbed her again, pulled her into a tight hug, and held her for a long time.

Finally she said, "Girta, your friends are only repeating what they hear in their own homes. You see, their mommies and daddies repeat what they heard from their own mommies and daddies. If you were to ask them why they said what they did, they wouldn't even know." She held Girta at arms length, "Listen to this and say it when they call you names. Okay?"

Girta nodded. Mother continued, "Sticks and stones may break my bones, but names will never hurt me."

Girta brightened, smiled, and asked, "May I go out and play now?" Her mother smiled back and nodded. "Yes."

If only real life were that simple!!

That limerick satisfied the little girl, but words do hurt us. Words *have* the power to injure or heal. They can create life in our spirits or they can produce death.

The tongue has power of life and death (Proverbs 18:21).

A lying tongue hates those it wounds and crushes, and a flattering mouth works ruin (Proverbs 26:28).

When I was very young, I loved to go the YMCA. One day I overheard an argument between the red-haired director and my brother-in-law, and they argued about me. The director said, "Don't much care whether he's all there mentally or not. I'll never use him on any of my teams." I left the building and never went back. Those words cut me to the core. *The tongue that brings healing is a tree of life, but a deceitful tongue crushes the spirit* (Proverbs 15:4).

Negativity and criticism can do more to wound and bruise the spirit than even physical violence.

As a small child, when I did something wrong, I was always reminded that I had two older brothers and they would not act like I just did. My mother wanted to motivate me to better behavior, but it backfired, causing only shame and humiliation. I lived most of my childhood under that banner of negativity and criticism.

I grew up, and after I graduated from high school I went into the Navy. I was converted while I was in the Navy, and when I was discharged I went to Bible School, but failed miserably. To make things worse, the school president called me into his office and said I'd never make it as a preacher. He said I was stupid and should find other work, but certainly not in the ministry. Those words wounded me deeply, shattering my hope, and to this day, when the enemy wants to taunt me, he brings those words to my mind.

Someone has said, "If in doubt, don't." If only we could recall that phrase before we speak! In fact, unkind and abrupt words can, over time, be considered verbal abuse.

ABUSE

Abuse takes three different forms; verbal, physical and sexual.

Verbal abuse is a sad part of our culture. It is all too common to hear people ridiculing children, spouses or even strangers. Verbal mudslinging is particularly harmful when it comes from those to whom we are close, those who should be the most supportive and encouraging. If you tell or even infer to a child that he is worthless, it becomes part of his belief system, and he grows up to exactly fulfill that prophecy. This is the awful legacy of verbal abuse.

I am reminded of the boy who brought a report card home with all A's and only one B. His father berated him for his less than perfect score, emphasizing only the B, and never even acknowledging the A's, causing the boy to feel that he would never measure up, no matter how well he did. *Scorn has broken my heart and hath left me helpless. I looked for sympathy, but there was none, for comforters, but I found none (Psalm 69:20).*

Physical violence is a major feature in the entertainment industry—on television, in videos and in the theaters. Media reports of real and widespread physical abuse are ever before us. Young children are injured, wives beaten, and innocent victims are attacked on the streets. I call this media barrage "Operation Saturation". When you see this violence often enough and over an extended period of time, it doesn't seem so bad after all and we accept it as truth. This is a lie from the pit of hell.

...the unfaithful have a craving for violence (Proverb 13:2).

Sexual Abuse

Sexual abuse, rape, homosexuality and incest are also major problems within our society. Because of the intimate nature of these forms of abuse, they are frequently concealed or denied. As a consequence, its victims are denied justice, and the guilty escape blame. To ignore such abuses is debasing to the victims.

In the Old Testament, the book of 1 Samuel tells the story of how Ammon, the son of David, became infatuated with and raped his half-sister Tamar. Over her protests, her brother, Absolom, convinced her to conceal the assault. *And Tamar lived in her brother Absolom's house, a desolate woman* (2 Samuel 13:20).

In times of sexual abuse, there is a great need for support. If this is not forthcoming, there is a strong sense of isolation and hopelessness. Without this support, innocent victims will frequently end up blaming themselves and languish in the guilt, which rightly belongs to another. This is what makes child molestation such a heinous sin. A vulnerable child is often abused by a close and trusted relative or friend, who then warns them to keep it their little secret. The child knows that what has happened is wrong, but there is no one to turn to for support. The child's life goes on, but with innocence lost and the guilt of sin now ever before them. Somehow, while trying to sort it all out, they may begin to feel that it was their fault and blame themselves for something that should not have happened in the first place.

One of my most wonderful experiences as a counselor with the Lehigh Valley Christian Counseling Service was with a woman who came for counseling and she refused to stop crying. A frustrated fellow counselor finally came to me and said, "This is our third session and I can't get her to talk. All she does is cry." I went into the counseling room with him and addressed her by name, asking who had sexually abused her.

At that point, she stopped crying, wiped her eyes, sat up, and began to talk.

Her mom died, and because she was the oldest girl, her dad used her as a wife, warning her never to tell what they did in secret. She carried this secret for years, until it surfaced, haunting her life, until she finally had to deal with it. Our Wonderful Counselor healed her completely. Sexual immorality is, in fact, a leading cause of damage to a wounded spirit.

Every wrong relationship can do damage to our spirit. But the Bible differentiates, separating sexual sins from all other sins (1 Corinthians 6:15-20).

Christians are joined to the Lord as *one spirit* (v.7).

Sexual immorality joins us to the body of the other sexual party. It affects every part of our being: spiritual, physical, and emotional. The conscience and sense of emotional equilibrium are shattered. 1 Corinthians 6:18 says, *Flee from sexual immorality. All other sins a man commits are outside the body, but he who sins sexually sins against his own body.*

A woman came to me in church one day, saying the Holy Spirit told her to leave her husband and marry the pastor. I couldn't hide my shock at the idea. I asked what her husband thought about this idea.

She said, "He said that if it's the will of God, who is he to stand in my way."

In holy boldness, I told the woman that God does not work that way. I suggested that she try the spirits to learn their source. The Bible says that adultery has its consequences. In Proverbs 6:32-35 (from the Living Bible), *But the man who commits adultery is an utter fool, for he destroys his own soul. Wounds and constant disgrace are his lot...* Solomon saw this first hand from his father David.

NOTE: For the innocent party in an adulterous affair. You did nothing wrong, so do not allow the enemy to lay false guilt on you. The enemy is Satan, the devil. If you let him, he will say that it's your fault; that you should have been a better spouse or a better daughter, and you are to blame in some other way.

After my wife of twenty-two years left our marriage, I searched in vain to learn what I had done wrong and eventually came to the conclusion that she had simply made a choice—a choice that had little to do with me, except that I had to live with the consequences.

The truth is, none of us is responsible for the choices of others. The only behavior we control is our own, so we need not feel guilty when wronged by another person. We can reassure ourselves, knowing God will ultimately hold them accountable for their choices. The Bible says, *Do not be deceived; God is not mocked; for whatsoever a man sows, that shall he also reap. For he that sows to his flesh shall of the flesh reap corruption; but he who sows to the spirit shall of the spirit reap life everlasting* (Galatians 6:7-8). We can trust God to vindicate us if we've been wronged, but only if we give up our control of the situation to the One who is sovereign.

NOTE: When in counseling, it should only be undertaken with someone of the same sex. That is, it is wisdom that men should counsel men and women counsel women. If, for some reason, men counsel women, or the reverse is true, *without exception*, another person must also be present in the room.

When people go for counseling, they are already in a most vulnerable state. It is then that the counselor, with the guidance of the Holy Spirit, invites the person to bare his/her soul. When addressing deep personal issues, intimacy often occurs between counselor and counselee. If the two are of the same gender, a warm bond forms, and healing begins. If, on the other hand, the counselor and counselee are of both sexes, this same bond can transform from admiration and gratitude into sexual attraction, easily misinterpreted as love, and a new and untenable relationship begins, out from under the blessing of God.

REJECTION BY THE LEADERSHIP

Let me tell you about a friend I met in seminary. He'd been born blind. He was an excellent scholar, and with the use of Braille and a high tech tape recorder, he excelled in college.

He had a love for Jesus that made you want to be like him. We became close friends when he asked me to read for him. With a sense of humor, he told me that if I continued to read so slowly, we would both be in seminary until Jesus came. I learned to read faster because his energy was catching.

When my friend graduated from college he applied for a church in his denomination. They did choose some men from his class to fill pulpits in their churches, but told him he needed to go to seminary. So there he was, and he put 125 percent into everything he did. He finished seminary with honors, but when he reapplied for a pastorate, the church leaders said, "Sorry, we don't want a blind man to preach in our churches."

In his case, broken promises led to a broken heart and a wounded spirit. And though the church had no place for him, the Lord has since used him mightily as an evangelist.

The truth is—hurting people hurt people.

A friend divulges a confidence or spreads an untruth about us. A promise is broken or hurtful words are spoken to us in anger. Those who take advantage of us, misuse us, or are simply difficult to deal with cause many ongoing problems.

My mother used to say, "Consider the source," if one of her children's feelings were hurt by someone else. And she was right. Ninety percent of the time, if we will consider the source, we will find that the perpetrator is the one who is hurting deep inside. The good news is—Jesus knows all about our hurts, because He was hurt, misunderstood, scorned, and finally, betrayed. He knows the people who hurt Him were also hurting, and that's why He said from the cross, *Father, forgive them, for they know not what they do* (Luke 23:34).

I found the Lord while I was in the Navy and also got married. But when I got out of the Navy I attended college under the GI Bill, which allowed us to live in relative comfort for the first couple of years. When, during my last year, the financial aid ceased, I worked two jobs while going to school. During that time, my wife was hospitalized for three months, which also left me in charge of our five-year-old son, Daniel.

Though it was a struggle, God was faithful, allowing me to graduate with two majors, one in Bible and another in Education. Shortly, I received a call to preach on a regular but temporary basis for a church that eventually hired me as their pastor, and I could scarcely contain my excitement at the prospect of my first congregation. Several Christian brothers tried to warn me of problems in this church, but I refused to listen. Even my denominational superintendent tried to forewarn me, but in my zeal, I would hear nothing negative, believing God would work things out. In truth, I refused the counsel of wise men to my detriment.

Overjoyed with my first preaching assignment, I felt happy and fulfilled in my new position. I grew to love the people and ministering to their needs. Each week, I preached twice on Sunday, as well as at Wednesday night prayer meeting and a weekly nursing home service. I even shared the responsibility of preaching over the radio once every few months. I couldn't help but be excited as the church grew over the next eighteen months, though they could only pay me a meager twenty-five dollars a week in salary.

Because I had a family to support, I applied for and took a position as a social worker for the Bureau of Children's Services in a small town in New Jersey. The pay was good, but the job required a significant time commitment. I want you to know the church was my first love, I felt disappointed at having to spend an inordinate amount of time at my secular job.

The job required me to investigate child abuse as a part of Child Protective Services. It offered opportunities to share God's love, and on occasion I saw people give their hearts to Christ. On one such occasion, I investigated a report from a school, regarding a child with multiple bruises. The father was apparently beating the child, egged on by her mother, who got a vicarious and sadistic thrill from the experience. After I shared the gospel with them, the husband accepted Christ and became a changed man. His wife, however, was unhappy with his new disposition, and called my office to complain. As a result, I was out of a job within days.

By the grace of God, I was unemployed less than a week, when I was hired as the caretaker for a cemetery, freeing up the time I needed to minister to my congregation. In this manner, the first year there went well and the church grew, but the denomination was undergoing reconstruction, with plans to merge with another denomination.

At the higher levels of leadership, the merger seemed a good thing, well thought-out and prayerfully considered, but the trickle-down effect proved much more difficult. On the district level, there were many misunderstandings and much discord.

Due to a ripple effect, I was feeling the discomfort of change and not for the better. In fact, my overseer was a man whose preaching was unequaled, except, unfortunately, by his grasping for power. The bottom line, as far as he was concerned, was whether the churches were adding to the denominational coffers. If not, he put them on a year's probation, to see if they could become profitable. If they didn't turn a profit within the specified time, they were to be closed, no questions asked.

When he looked at our church's financial records, he only saw red ink. When he asked if I could be willing to stay another year, I agreed, and asked if he would keep it open if it was no longer a burden on the district. He didn't exactly agree, but neither did he say no, so our little church assumed the responsibility for the mortgage, to relieve the district of the financial burden, hoping to remain a viable church body. As the Lord blessed, the church continued to grow, and peoples' lives were being changed, until our books showed a 100 percent increase in overall income. I was excited to be part of a move of God, and was hopeful about its future.

One internal faction caused ongoing problems. A single individual, a power-wielding woman, tried in every way she could, to run the church. Though I was kind, I never played into her hands, which made her very angry, so when she couldn't manipulate me, she found an easier mark in my wife, confronting her regarding unnecessary and fussy issues, such as how to hang the toilet tissue and the length of my wife's hair and dresses. Before long, I could no longer ignore the strain, though I never confronted the woman head on.

When my district superintendent came for his yearly visit and heard what was happening, it was all the excuse he needed, and he simply told me the church would be closed. I felt a staggering sense of disappointment and disillusionment, after taking on all the financial obligations and struggling so hard to make it work.

To add insult to injury, he replaced me before the closing date with a seminary student, and assigned me to oversee the denominational campgrounds, reducing my already low pay, and requiring me to fill the pulpit when other pastors had to be absent. Anxious about my deteriorating financial situation, I asked how much the pay would be for filling the pulpit. His face reddened and he shouted, "What you get is what you get. Are you never satisfied?" I was so shocked that I didn't answer, but recalled hearing that his own request for extra pay for preaching over and above his normal obligations had been approved without hesitation. At that point, I remembered an incident that had happened earlier. Because of his gifted preaching ministry, I had once asked if he would come and preach at our church, to which he laughed out loud. "No, Bob. You can't pay me enough to come to that little church."

Though I knew it was happening, I couldn't help but sink into depression after my demotion from the position of pastor to that of a lowly caretaker.

After a time, we settled into a new church, pastored by a former college professor of mine, and began helping with the Wednesday night youth ministry. One night the pastor's wife, who was in charge of the youth, became upset with those she considered rowdy, and shouted harshly at them. Afterward, I mentioned that I thought she was a bit tough on them and suggested she might want to try to relax. Not long after, her husband, the pastor—evidently angered about the incident—called me in and demanded I leave his church and never return. Feeling sick, misunderstood and humiliated, I wept all the way back to camp. In reality, I felt like I was drowning, going down for the third time, never to rise again.

Our rocky financial situation made it necessary for me to take a second job, and I mentioned to my superintendent that I had taken a job at our local McDonald's Restaurant to make ends meet. I felt the familiar lump in the pit of my stomach when he frowned in annoyance. He said succinctly, "If you had more faith in God, you wouldn't be having this problem with finances." When I responded that my faith in God was not paying my bills, fury flashed in his eyes, and I couldn't help but wonder what I was doing wrong. It's hard to admit, but I was disappointed in myself and yet angry with him. He'd made it sound so simple. And if that was the case, why was it never that easy for me?

During this time, I was filling the pulpit for a pastor who was very ill. When he was up to it, he would come to the service and hear me preach, and often, he and his wife would have my family over for Sunday dinner, after which I would return to preach the evening service. The schedule of preaching and holding down two jobs was by then wearing me down both physically and emotionally. After a time, the pastor regained his health and reclaimed his pulpit for a time, and I was relieved to return to a more relaxed schedule that included only McDonald's and my camp duties. Not long afterward, he once against became ill, and I resumed preaching in his place. Because he was too sick to attend, his wife came alone, and it was soon clear that her attitude toward me had changed. When he called me in for a visit shortly thereafter, he lambasted me for preaching what his wife had called the worst Calvinistic sermon she had ever heard. He demanded that I leave and never return.

By now, I was weary in body and spirit, discouraged after another confrontation as well as from raking leaves from six a.m. to two p.m., and then working at McDonald's from three to eleven, in a place reminiscent of my college years, burning the candle at both ends and losing hope for the future. It was all I could do to put one foot in front of the other and keep going. I tried to be grateful that I was still employed, not realizing that even that would soon end.

Time for a pastoral conference was approaching, though I wasn't planning to go because of lack of finances, and the trip was two and a half hours away. My DS and four other pastors did go and, as happens, people talk. Apparently, I was a major topic of conversation on the way to the conference.

After conference, I was called into the district superintendent's office, where he announced, "You Wesleyans just don't cut it. Pastor …'s wife said… you preached a Calvinist sermon. I'll not have a Calvinist preaching in any of my pulpits. You'll never preach here again."

When I tried to explain, and asked if he would read my sermon, he refused and said, "My mind is already made up.

Once again I was out of a job, this time not just out of the pulpit, but no longer even the camp caretaker. I felt humiliated and devastated by the blow of his angry words. Awash in despair, I struggled for a reason to go on. I was the end product of gossip

The word gossip is an interesting word. It stems from the root word meaning godparent or close friend. The person who gossips has to be close enough to know and share personally the damaging details of another's life. When you are a Christian, and especially in ministry, you expose yourself, becoming vulnerable, close to those in your circle. And if they gossip, chatting idly or spreading rumors about your affairs, it feels like a wound in the heart, and can make you cautious, even fearful, about sticking your neck out again.

With the end of my caretaker's job looming large before us, we would shortly have nowhere to live. What money we had managed to save, which was minimal, would be gone very quickly. To tell the truth, I was becoming afraid of God. Voicing my thoughts out loud, I looked up and yelled, "Are you deserting me too?" If He heard my question, He gave no indication. I should have known He had other plans.

The very next day, my wife called me in from painting garbage cans (see any irony here?) to answer the phone. The director of a nearby rescue mission asked me to come to work there as soon as we could make arrangements to move.

I explained that we needed a place to live, and he said that would be no problem. In fact, my salary would include housing and be more than I received from my church district. God is good and has every detail worked out for us in our lives. If only we could trust and obey day by day!

CHAPTER TWO

Crucified by Christians

Even during the long years of heartache, I knew in my head that God was sovereign. I had even preached on the subject, but it was difficult, if not impossible, to see how it would all together for good.

Gene Edwards wrote a book entitled, *Have You Been Crucified By Christians?* Please get the book and read it in its entirety, but here is a synopsis of the book.

Some Christians have been grievously mistreated by other believers. Some are so severely mistreated that it amounts to a crucifixion.

Being crucified by fellow Christians is one of the deepest pains a child of God will ever know. It can so profoundly affect you that it can mark the end of your life as a practicing Christian.

Place your crucifixion in the realm of the invisible, in realms unseen. Only there will you truly find the person who deliberately caused you to be crucified. Only in the realm of the spirituals will you find the perpetrator. When you were crucified at the hands of men, in reality you but entered into a crucifixion. Consider the circumstances, which led to His crucifixion. Who caused His cross, His crucifixion? Who was it that plotted His Golgotha? It was exactly the same person who plotted yours. That person actually designed that you enter into your Lord's *sufferings*. After all, you the believer are in Him.

The Father willed His own Son's crucifixion. And yours. Refusal to accept your crucifixion as wholly from the hand of God only means you were not crucified, you were mistreated. Only when you accept that it came from God…only then is it a true crucifixion. *The crucifixion of a Christian comes from the hand of God, and God alone.*

You must find a whole new view of your crucifixion. There was far more purpose in it than you realized. Perhaps far more good in its content than you can presently imagine.

What happened to you was meant to be a magnificent beginning of transformation in your life. The circumstances which birthed this tragedy were exactly what you needed. That hellish event brought you to exactly the place your Lord wants you to be.

God is omnipotent, totally in control of all that happens to us as His children. He knew I needed all these experiences so that I can say with the Apostle Paul, *To the weak, I became weak, to win the weak. I have become all things to all men, so that by all possible means I might save some* (1 Corinthians 9:22 NIV).

This is not the same old argument between the Calvinist and Armenian camps that can't resolve how much of life happens because of God's control or lack of it.

In this case, our loving heavenly Father knows the beginning, the middle and the end of the story, and all of it simultaneously. He watches over us with a steadfast and unwavering eye. Every move is monitored, every tear counted. According to scripture, my Father knows what I need even before I ask for it. My heavenly Father knows when a sparrow falls, counts the number of hairs on my head, and enters into my pain and injury, using it to draw me to Himself, and ultimately changing me into a reflection of His character.

The truth, when I could finally understand it, was that God did not orchestrate what happened to me, but He did allow it to take its course, planning to turn around what the enemy meant for harm, and use it for my good.

God, in His omniscience, knows the direction we will take, before we ever take it, as well as whether it's right or wrong. But because of His grace, which never fails, He also always provides a detour back to righteousness if and when we are ready to take it. I'm going to be honest here and confess that I have a terrible sense of direction when it comes to driving on superhighways. Somehow I can read a sign and still make the wrong turn. But I find it reassuring that I can always get off at the nearest exit, turn around and get back on track. And it's the same way with God, who never, ever gives up on His kids.

CHAPTER THREE

The Rescue Mission

By the time I started working at the Rescue Mission, I was a little gun shy with regard to Christians and the church, but felt grateful for a new start.

We moved into the apartment supplied by the mission, a small space, with five rooms in a row, each one leading into another, and all open.

We put up bookshelves to divide the spaces into sections, for more privacy. And now that we had a place to live, we had a bit of space to entertain guests, which was good, since my wife, Carolyn was very family oriented—so much so that we usually had one or more of her family living with us.

I married while I was in the Navy. Shortly after my discharge from the Navy we had a son, Daniel Edward. He was the greatest thing that ever happened in my life except for Jesus Christ saving me. He was number one son.

We had the rooms arranged so that we had the room off the bathroom as our bedroom and initially Danny took the room next door, but not for long. Carolyn's niece, Cindy, moved in. Cindy's mom and dad were having marital problems so she came to live with us. Now Danny moved into what had been the dining room, which meant we squeezed into the kitchen for meals.

While I was pasturing a church in Neptune, New Jersey, we had a foster son. He was about a year older than Danny and we loved him as our own son. When we moved back to Pennsylvania, he did not come along but stayed with his mother. When we were settled at the Mission he wrote me a heart wrenching letter which, bottom line, said he missed us and wanted to come live with his new family. He moved in and shared a room with Danny.

To say that life was hectic at this point is a vast understatement, as Cindy wasn't happy with us and living according to our rules. Often either Carolyn or I was called to school because of Cindy's behavior, which kept the entire household in a state of perpetual upheaval. Even after spending an inordinate amount of time and money for counseling for her, things did not improve. Danny and Ted were feeling the strain between Carolyn and me.

Three years later, Cindy persuaded her dad to let her live with him. But by then, the damage was done, and the boys, especially Danny, rebelled at what he considered his parents' neglect, and consoled himself with drugs and bad company. Ted enlisted in the Navy, and Carolyn and I were once again alone.

CHAPTER FOUR

The Empty Nest

I'm sure you are familiar with the 'empty nest syndrome.' This is the time when a married couple has finished raising their children, and one by one, they all leave home to start their own life.

With the children gone, Carolyn was bored, so she took a job in the rescue mission thrift store, while I worked three nights and one day of every weekend. As sometimes happens, we grew apart. In the course of her work, Carolyn got acquainted with one of the mission residents who worked at the store. In the process of counseling him, they grew close, then fell in love. When he left the mission, she went with him, leaving me alone after twenty-two years of marriage. Because of her departure, most of our friends were too uncomfortable with the situation to have anything to do with me, and I felt very much alone and shattered. I had choices to make. Would I let this trial destroy me, or try to get past it?

With a need to keep busy, I asked the mission superintendent for all the extra hours I could get and threw myself into my work. When I wasn't busy working, I read everything I could get my hands on. I got books from the mission's thrift shop and read at least two or more each week. Then it occurred to me that if I was going to go to all the trouble to learn, I might as well study with a goal in mind and work toward my master's degree. I applied and was accepted into seminary, and threw myself into my studies.

This should have been the best time of my life, but sin has a way of taking what is good and making it play havoc in our lives. Bad choices on my part took me out of God's divine will, and I have no one to blame but myself. My life went downhill at this point in time,

CHAPTER FIVE

No Reason to Live

I was still at the mission, struggling to regain my emotional balance. In my mind and heart I was thinking things couldn't get worse. But they did.

The superintendent's wife, a loving and caring godly woman whom everyone loved, died suddenly, stunning everyone and leaving her husband alone and hurting bad. I only realized how devastated he felt one morning in devotions at the mission, when I heard him say the most painful words I had ever heard in my life. He said, "I think God made a mistake. He took my wife and let Bob live." That was a gunshot wound to the bone. With a feeling of horror and embarrassment I can not start to describe, I felt like I would die right then and there. Though I would rather have never seen him again, it was my job to make daily pick-ups in the mission truck, and I had to get my assigned destinations from him. There was no eye contact between us when I asked, "So God made a mistake, huh?" He countered with, "Well, she lived a good life and was never divorced." That was all that was said. Clearly, he had no remorse for his hurtful words.

It was all I could do to finish my morning pick-ups before I essentially ran away from home, driven off by my feelings of self-loathing and embarrassment. For the umpteenth time in my life, a brother in the Lord expressed hatred for me, and I had to ask myself—Did God feel the same way? Feeling desperately alone, I left without notice and hitchhiked to my mother's house, 150 miles away. But I found no solace there, and because I couldn't stay forever, I returned to the only place I called home. Needless to say, I didn't continue to work at the Mission very long after this. I left the Mission and was completely on my own. Now I had no job, no home, no friends, and almost no money. I had sunken to the depths of despair, sleeping in my car. I could go nowhere for help, so alienated was I at that time in my life. I prayed to God that He would let me get pneumonia so I could die.

As low as I was, I could see God working in my life, when, after living in my car for a week, I found a sales job that paid well, but only on commission. Though sales were sparse, I was able to rent a room in an inexpensive residential motel, some know it as a *flop house,* and had money enough to feed myself.

CHAPTER SIX

Wandering Far from God

I was born into a wonderful home, went into the Navy and accepted Jesus Christ as my Savior. When I got out of the Navy I went to Bible School and went into the ministry. Some would say that I had it made on planet earth. But the struggle went on. Like a soldier on the battle front, I got careless and was wounded. I was taken out of action for a while.

With all I had ever held dear on the line, I lost my will to survive, and staggered into a world where nothing mattered, including whether or not I held onto righteousness. I became one with the world. As hard as it is to admit, I began doing the very things I had preached against, as a born-again, evangelical Christian pastor. For a time, I kept reading my Bible, and tried to pray, but it felt as if my prayers were bouncing off the ceiling, unheard. Even in my confusion, I knew I needed to get right with God, but because I was angry with Him for what felt like abandonment, it wasn't hard to ignore Him and go my own way.

Because I have always felt a deep sense of personal fulfillment from my work as a pastor and counselor, I felt a corresponding deep sense of loss when that avenue of service was gone.

With a need to support myself and get back on my feet, I once again applied for and got a job in human services, working in a group home, caring for mentally handicapped adults. Because I needed a place to stay and they needed an overnight charge person, I moved in and made it my home. Though most people would not welcome living in such a place, it was a definite improvement over my flophouse existence.

Struggling to regain my sense of self worth, I settled into the routine, and found that I was accepted by my charges. The atmosphere there lent itself beautifully to recovery. Before long, I was given more responsibility, and realized I was finally beginning to heal.

Then the Lord did something wonderful, bringing a kind, godly woman named Marian to work with me. Spending time together, Marian and I learned that we shared many similar, difficult experiences. Simply talking through the pain seemed to bring relief, and after a time, we grew to love each other and were married.

As I slowly regained my sense of emotional balance, I threw myself into my work and my marriage 100 percent, but there was a nagging in my spirit that I just couldn't ignore. I was searching for intimacy with God. He was the prodigal's Father and saying, "Come back to Me?" This left open the chance of meeting anyone with an authentic relationship with Him.

In that frame of mind, I met a man who was starting a Christian counseling service, and after a time, I assumed some of the counseling responsibilities. Unfortunately, my theology was at odds with his, and discussion after discussion failed to resolve the gaping chasm between us. I simply stayed because they needed me there.

Then one day I was asked to speak at one of the prayer meetings. I began by saying, "Today, we're going back to the basics," by which I meant the doctrine of sin, salvation and how to live in righteousness. One woman stood and yelled, "We don't need the basics. We need to know more about the gifts!" Trying to be gentle and low key, I addressed her comment, asking her to please sit down and be respectful—that if she preferred to be disrespectful, I would have an usher escort her to the door. She sat down and didn't say another word. The counseling service, by now, was disintegrating, built, as it was, on the sinking sand of foundationless name-it-claim-it doctrines of men. It closed shortly thereafter, once again leaving me with a sense of personal failure.

We had enjoyed and now missed the counseling ministry, and without giving it much thought, opened one of our own. But, because it, too, was built on the foundation of man's imagination and not in the heart of God, it quickly failed. After so many rejections, I withdrew, scooting away to lick my wounds, thinking it couldn't possibly get much worse—that I had already reached the end of the line. The pain of failure and abandonment was like a sore that would never heal, coloring the way I looked at life. In fact, death looked like a real and welcome form of escape.

Here's what David Wilkerson, a man of God with a heart for drug addicts, has to say regarding being at the end of one's rope.

> Why do we feel like giving up at times? Mostly because we act as if God has forsaken the earth. We don't doubt His existence or His reality, but our prayers seem to go unanswered. We cry for His help, in such desperation, and He seems not to hear. We struggle along, making one mistake after another.
>
> We make promises to do better; we get into the Bible; we cry and pray and stay busy helping others and doing good. But we are so often left with an empty, unfulfilled sensation. The promises of God haunt us.
>
> We claim those promises in what we believe is honest, childlike faith, but time after time, we fail to receive what we ask for. In the hour of temptation, down we go.
>
> Doubt creeps in, and Satan whispers, "Nothing works. In spite of your tears, prayers and trust in God's Word, nothing really changes. Days, weeks and even years go by, and your prayers, hopes and dreams are still unanswered and unfulfilled. Quit! Give up!"
>
> Every Christian on this planet reaches that crisis point at one time or another in life. And in that moment, when the walls seem to be caving in and the roof seems to be collapsing, when everything seems to be coming apart and sin demands the upper hand, a voice deep within cries out, "Walk away from it all. Pack it in! Escape! Why put up with it? Run away. You don't have to take it. Do something drastic."[3]

This scenario describes my situation exactly. When I was at the end of my resources, I gave the enemy an opening to come in and destroy what little remained. With this new knowledge, questions flooded my mind, and I asked God why He would force me to go through all this. Had I lived a lie all these years? Why had He let me down just when I needed Him the most? No matter how hard I tried, I could not seem to get a handle on it. From outward appearances, it may have seemed that I was living in God's will at that time, but I was not experiencing intimacy with God.

A preacher from Ireland visited the church one Sunday night, and stopped abruptly in the middle of his sermon and asked, "Now, Lord?"

I was always skeptical when a preacher prophesied over people, so I thought, *Oh no, here we go again.* My mind was wandering when suddenly I heard him call my name, that quickly got my attention and I sat up to hear his words. He said, "Robert, the Lord says it's happening again, but the end is better than the beginning." That was it; end of prophecy. As you can imagine, I was dumbfounded to think God would be speaking to me in such a personal way. But suddenly I wanted to hear more, so as soon as possible, I got out my Bible and began searching for answers. Interestingly enough, I found his exact prophecy in the last chapter of the book of Job, clearly confirming the man's words. It was obvious that the Lord wanted my undivided attention, and His words have remained in my heart over the years, sustaining me through further times of struggle.

One warning regarding prophecy is that it must be confirmed in some way—either in scripture or by another source. God's Word demands that we test the spirits. In fact, the prophecies of Old Testament prophets were confirmed only if what they prophesied came to pass.

You might wonder how the church in our day regards those who are suffering. Though the church was there during my struggles, its emphasis was on other things, and it wasn't really willing to weep when we, my wife and I, wept or support us in our heartache. In fact, our friends didn't want to know that we were hurting, because it demanded that they do something. When they did finally learn of our difficulties, most were simply there to offer easy solutions to untenable problems, and they quickly grew impatient when their solutions proved ineffective and unworkable. Often we were told to "just snap out of it," but that proved humanly impossible. We had come to a place where we didn't fit into their theology at all.

Quoting David Wilkerson again–

God didn't promise to give you a painless way of life; He promised you a way of escape. He promised to help you bear your pain and give you strength to put you back on your feet when weakness makes you stagger.

Most likely you did what you had to do. You moved in the will of God, honestly following your heart. You went into it with an open heart, willing to give of yourself. Love was your motivation. You did not abort the will of God; someone else did. If that were not true, you would not be the one hurting so. You are hurt because you tried to be honest.

You can't understand why things blew up in your face, when God seemed to be leading all along. Your heart asks, "Why did God allow me to get into this in the first place if He knew it would never work out right? But the answer is clear. Judas was called by the Lord; he was destined to be a man of God. He was hand picked by the Savior; he could have been mightily used by God. But Judas aborted God's plan. He broke the heart of Jesus. What started out as a beautiful, perfect plan of God ended in disaster, because Judas chose to go his own way. Pride and stubbornness wrecked the plan of God that was in operation.

So lay off the guilt trips. Stop condemning yourself. Stop trying to figure out what you did wrong. It is what you are thinking right now that counts with God. You did not make a mistake; more than likely, you simply gave too much. Like Paul, you have to say, "The more I loved you, the less I be loved" (see 2 Corinthians 12:15)[4].

CHAPTER SEVEN

How Low Can You Sink?

God is a good God. He promises to never leave nor forsake His children. Like the father on the housetop, He was waiting for His prodigal to return. I was that prodigal child.

Just as He was with the biblical prodigal while he slopped the hogs and ate their food, He was beside me as I did janitorial work in the church, and He whispered into my heart this question. "If I ordained you to preach the gospel, what are you doing cleaning toilets? Not that there is anything wrong with being a servant if the need arises, but in my case, I felt unworthy to do anything more valuable than clean toilets and saw no way out of the present miserable situation. Believe it or not, I even applied for a job running after garbage trucks, picking up other peoples' garbage. In the end, I didn't get the job, but I heard the Holy Spirit impress on me again, "This is not what you worked so hard to achieve, nor what I have called you to do."

I was in God's permissive will while I excelled as the house supervisor for the group home, a period of ten years, before it became an ongoing struggle just to continue on.

Marian kept her job as supervisor of her group home, when I finally retired early, at 62, and began collecting Social Security. She earned a decent wage, allowing us to relax and enjoy our lives for the very first time since our marriage. That is, until it all fell apart.

Marian had worked a sixteen-hour shift on a Saturday, so on Sunday morning we went out for breakfast and then spent time going to garage sales. We ended up at a farmer's market and flea market. After shopping for a time, Marian excused herself because she was getting tired, saying she would wait in the van while I finished looking around. She had nearly reached our vehicle when the van from her group home pulled into the parking lot. Thrilled to see Marian, her affectionate charges flew out of the van, and one man ran up to give her an excited hug. In the process, however, he lifted his feet off the ground, and Marian was left holding a 150 pound man, whose weight broke her back. I was just returning to the van when I saw her bent over and in excruciating pain.

Once at home, she took something for pain and went to lie down, where she stayed the rest of the day and through the long, painful night that followed. When morning came, she was in severe pain, but insisted upon going to work. Unable to continue after a few hours at work, she came home early, and was never able to work again.

This circumstance changed our lives forever. Without Marian being able to go to work and bring in an income, I went through an agency and was shortly hired as a home health aid, to care for an attorney who had been severely brain-injured in an auto accident.

Through his firm, we were able to get legal representation for Marian, but as it turned out, they also represented her employer, which resulted in a minimal settlement for Marian's permanent and life-altering injuries. Though she underwent back surgery, she is still in constant daily pain.

Once again, we had been wronged, this time by a secular organization. It could've caused us to once again lose hope, but now we see things in a different light.

We serve a great big, wonderful God, who never leaves or abandons us, but neither does he force Himself upon us. He allows us to go our own way if that is our desire. But *His* desire is that we return to Him, giving Him our complete and undivided attention.

Part II

Biblical Characters' Wounds and Healings

In his book, *Rebuilding Your Broken World*, author Gordon MacDonald compares our own shattering life experiences to disaster films, where we are suddenly threatened and our lives are irrevocably and negatively changed by forces from either inside or outside of ourselves.

> Out of these cinematic metaphors I first conceived the phrase *broken world* as an apt way to describe what happens when someone sustains a major blow in life that is either self-inflicted or the result of someone else's unfortunate or treacherous performance. I'm thinking of disasters in the inner spirit, to the mind, to the body, to relationships, to reputations, or to personal usefulness.
>
> …personal words are in many cases remarkable fragile, and they can shatter under stress much like an elegant goblet explodes under a barrage of powerful sound waves. I call people like that *broken world people*.
>
> …when one's world has been broken, the question of hope usually arises. Is there a tomorrow? Will there be a second chance? Is the damage permanent? Do new starts exist? Can the *broken world* ever be rebuilt? (Emphasis mine).[5]

Keeping this quote in mind, let's look at some biblical greats to see how they handled and ultimately recovered from devastating wounds.

CHAPTER EIGHT

Joseph

Joseph's life, detailed in the book of Genesis, can be summed up by three R's: rejection, response and resilience.

Even as a child, Joseph experienced rejection. Because his mother, Rachel, was the one real love of Jacob's life, her only son, Joseph, became his favorite son, causing his brothers terrible resentment, jealous of the special place he held in his father's heart.

To show him he loved him, Jacob fashioned an intricately woven, multicolored coat that set Joseph apart from his brothers. And because Joseph lived in his father's tent and received visible favoritism, his brothers quickly grew to despise him.

Joseph was part of the line that would produce the Savior, and God chose to reveal in a dream His plan to use Joseph in ministry. Unfortunately, Joseph unwisely shared this with his brothers, only fueling their rage.

One day, Joseph was sent to take lunch to his brothers who were tending sheep in the fields, and when they saw him coming, they hatched a plot to kill him and send his beautiful coat, covered with blood, back to their father. But his brother, Reuben, argued that, instead of taking Joseph's life, they should leave him in a pit, and the brothers agreed. Reuben planned to return for him later.

After stripping off Joseph's coat, they threw him in the pit, dipped his coat in blood, and set off for home, before shortly meeting a caravan headed to Egypt. Wanting to be rid of him, yet without the guilt of his blood on their consciences, the brothers sold him to a slave-trader in the caravan.

Can you empathize with Joseph's awful disappointment? After finding favor with both his father and God, and with the promise of a future of influence, he suddenly found himself in a pit and then sold as a slave, which certainly must have brought terrible confusion and despair.

Once in the city, the merchants sold Joseph as a slave to a man named Potiphar, and because he was young, strong and capable, Joseph was put in charge of the man's entire household of slaves. After trying and failing several times to seduce Joseph, Potiphar's wife cried rape, and Joseph was thrown into prison. No doubt confused and devastated by this latest turn of events, he had to wonder what God was doing.

While in prison, he gained the trust of those in authority and was put in charge of other prisoners. During this time, he developed a reputation as one who could interpret dreams. Two of the king's servants, the baker and the cupbearer (wine-taster) were thrown into jail, and in due time each had a dream, which no one but Joseph could interpret. Not long after, his interpretation came true, and the baker was put to death while the cupbearer returned to the palace, promising to recommend Joseph to the king. But as time went on and no word came from the king regarding Joseph's release, he must've felt heartsick, and had to wonder at the direction his life had taken.

Outside the prison walls, the king had a disturbing dream, which he demanded that his holy men interpret, although he couldn't recall any of its details or explain it in any way.

In spite of their best efforts, not one of them could interpret the dream, until the cupbearer recalled how Joseph had interpreted his dream years earlier. When Joseph was summoned, he was able to discern and interpret the dream, which foretold of seven years of plenty and another seven of famine to follow. He further urged the king to store up what he could during the good years, to keep them alive in the lean years, and so impressed the king that he named Joseph second in command and put him in charge of procurement of food.

The famine, when it came, was so far-reaching that it also affected the Children of Israel, including Joseph's family, and because they were in need of food, Jacob sent his sons to Egypt for provisions. When they arrived and Joseph saw them, his heart was troubled, but also touched by their need for food. Longing for that lost family connection, he said, "I am Joseph! Is my father still living?" But his brothers were not able to answer him, because they were terrified, condemned by the guilt of their sin. Then Joseph said to his brothers, "I am your brother Joseph, the one you sold into Egypt! And now do not be distressed and do not be angry with yourselves for selling me here, because it was to save lives that God sent me ahead of you. For two years now there has been a famine in the land, and for the next five years, there will not be plowing and reaping. But God sent me ahead of you to preserve for you a remnant on earth and to save your lives by a great deliverance. "So then it was not you who sent me here, but God. He made me father to Pharaoh, Lord of his entire household and ruler of all Egypt" (Genesis 45:3-8 NIV).

After what he had been through, Joseph could easily have given up, despairing of ever seeing the answer to God's promises. No doubt, he prayed to escape his difficult circumstances, but God didn't free him until the appointed time. In the middle of this trying situation, God met him where he was and encouraged him, using the trials to help break Joseph out of the prison of self.

In fact, when faced repeatedly with the decision to throw away his faith or trust to trust God, he chose to believe God, and every time he made that decision, God used those same tough circumstances to strengthen him, increasing his endurance and building his faith and maturity, and preparing him for greater things ahead.

It's interesting to note that nowhere in scripture does God speak negatively about Joseph. He repeatedly experienced crushing emotional wounds, but always chose to believe God, and could say as a testimony to his brothers that what they meant for evil, God brought forth as good.

CHAPTER NINE

Moses

H ere is a man with whom I can identify, perhaps because he was eighty years old before God chose to use him. This story gives me hope that God may be able to use me as well.

Moses experienced multiple broken world situations that could have caused him to quit, in which case no one would have been able to offer a word of criticism. I like to think of him as God's man with God's message to God's people in God's time.

Moses was born at a time when the Children of Israel were enslaved in Egypt. They were multiplying so fast that they became a threat to the power elite there. It simply wasn't good to have a greater population of slaves than of your own countrymen. Because of this perceived threat, Pharaoh put out a decree that all the male babies born to the Israelites were to be killed.

His mother, heartbroken over such a terrible edict, was desperate for a way to preserve the life of her son. Trusting in God, she wove a basket of rushes and sealed it with pitch, then placed her son inside and assigned his older sister, Miriam, to watch over it. They placed the basket in the area of the river where Pharaoh's daughter came to bathe, and the Lord caused the baby to cry just as she appeared for her bathing ritual. Touched by the baby's weeping, the princess rescued Moses and took him home to the palace to live as her son, and making a way for God's plan to continue against all odds.

We don't have many details of life in the palace, which makes me wonder how the royal family treated Moses, an interloping outsider. I wonder if the household accepted him as one of them, or continually threw at him the story of his birth. Could they have called him a dog (a derogatory term the Egyptians used to describe Jews) all the while he was living in the palace? I ask these questions because we see Moses wandering among the slaves of Egypt. What was he doing there? Was he searching for his biological mother? A good Egyptian would not have been caught in the presence of these sweaty, smelly slaves, but Moses spent time among them. At what point did he realize he was a Jew?

While spending time with the slaves, he observed a slave being unjustly treated and had compassion on him. So much so that he intervened in the altercation and ended up killing the perpetrator. The next day when he saw two Hebrew slaves fighting, he tried to break up the fight, and one of them yelled, "What are you going to do? Are you going to kill us like you did the Egyptian?" Once his secret was revealed, the now forty-year old Moses was forced to escape the area, simply to save his life. If Pharaoh learned he had killed an Egyptian, he could easily have ordered Moses killed, too, with no questions asked.

So where did this wealthy, educated man end up? On the backside of the desert, tending sheep that were not even his own. Picture this in your mind: Moses was raised and educated in the royal palace. He was looking for his roots, and when he tried to help his brothers and killed an Egyptian his life changed. Up to that point, Moses had lived his entire life in luxury in the palace of a king, until his world was shattered, and he could no longer feel safe or welcome at home.

Moses nursed his wounds for forty long years, and just at the time he had recovered, God chose to reveal Himself to this weary, downtrodden man. Moses was tending his sheep when the unimaginable happened. His brows must have furrowed at the sight of a bush on fire, but, amazingly, not being consumed by the flames. As he drew near the bush to study the situation, God spoke to him in an audible voice and told Moses to remove his shoes, for the ground on which he stood was holy ground.

It was God's inimitable call upon Moses' life, and that at the advanced age of eighty years old. God may have said something like this to Moses. "During the last forty years, you have matured, learning how to cope with painful life experiences. And now that you have recovered, I have a job for you to do. Go deliver My people from the land of Egypt."

After the burning bush experience, Moses accepted God's assignment, probably knowing it wouldn't be easy. In fact, Moses went to Pharaoh, requesting he set Israel free, and nine times his pleas fell on deaf ears. Putting ourselves in his shoes, it's easy to imagine how he might have felt like a fool, when the plan seemed a miserable failure. Each time Pharaoh rejected God's demand to free Israel, he essentially shot himself in the foot, already warned of the dire consequences that lay ahead.

The tenth and final terrible plague ended Pharaoh's opposition. By now, he was defeated and he knew it. He let Israel go, but shortly changed his mind, and sent his army out to capture them and bring them back. By the time Moses saw them coming, he and the Children of Israel were between the proverbial rock and the hard place, stranded between the Red Sea and the rapidly-approaching armies of Egypt. But the God of the burning bush answered the desperate prayer of Moses, and opened up the Red Sea, creating a huge wall of water on either side of dry ground, so that the Israelites could safely pass through.

Without a thought to his peril, an equally desperate Pharaoh charged after the Israelites, through the path in the Red Sea, where God brought the walls of water together, destroying every last Egyptian, including Pharaoh himself.

As he rejoiced over their freedom, Moses might've thought he had made it. Surely nothing could hurt him now. Not so.

After an awesome deliverance at the dividing of the Red Sea, he might've thought they would never again doubt God's awesome power. But the people continually challenged him, complaining over issues like a lack of water, or no variety of food. The doubting and complaining must have wounded Moses again, and probably made him feel like a failure. In fact, at times the Children of Israel were so angry with Moses that they considered stoning him. Over and over, he went to God for help in managing his ungrateful, demanding charges. But the most dramatic evidence of their wayward hearts was still yet to come.

God called Moses up to Mount Sinai, where the two communed and God fashioned the tablets containing the Ten Commandments. Before he left, Moses put his brother, Aaron in charge, and told him to keep the peace until he returned. But when Moses failed to return in what the people considered a significant length of time, they decided God had failed to keep His promises, and told Aaron they wanted his help to build a new god, this one more worthy of their worship. Too weak to argue with the people, Aaron told them to bring their gold jewelry, and when he had collected enough, he melted it down and built them a statue of a calf.

When Moses reappeared out of the mountain, he must've been shocked, seeing the people out of control, worshiping the calf as well as giving themselves to all sorts of sinful behavior. Furious at their debauchery, he threw down the tablets of the law and broke them.

"And he took the calf they had made and burned it in the fire; then he ground it to powder, scattered it on the water and made the Israelites drink it" (Exodus 32:19-21 NIV). The wayward behavior of the Israelites reflected badly on Moses every time it happened, and Moses himself ended up playing go-between on many occasions, simply to keep God from destroying them all in His anger.

Only a man with great strength of character could have continued on in light of all that occurred during the forty years in the wilderness. But even Moses had his limits, as we shall see.

The Children of Israel were quick to complain about everything, and this time was no exception. Not for the first time, they demanded water. Now they could have simply asked God in faith, but they didn't. In fact, they put Moses on the spot, and demanded that he make something happen immediately. God, who was patiently listening as Moses prayed about their need for water, immediately answered, telling him to simply speak to the rock, and it would produce the water they needed. You'll notice here that Moses has grown in grace, and where he used to have to strike the rock for it to begin to produce water, he now only had to speak to the rock for the water to begin flowing. But Moses, now furious with the people for their ungrateful, complaining spirit, and at the end of his rope, let his anger get the best of him, and struck the rock in disobedience to God's command. In doing so, Moses shot himself in the foot and paid a huge price for the privilege.

From God's point of view, there is no excuse for disobedience, not even when we are justifiably angered by someone else's sin. Moses learned this lesson the hard way, when God told him he would see but would never enter the Promised Land. He must have had great remorse for acting out in anger.

63

CHAPTER TEN

Job

The book of Job is at the direct center of the Bible, with easy access to its wisdom. I would venture to say that this book is used more in counseling than any other, because Job's life represents the epitome of a broken world. Many of us would not survive what Job experienced in such a short period of time. Within minutes, he went from riches to rags, from having it all to having nothing. When a pastor teaches about perseverance through trials, he often uses Job as the example of righteousness.

Just when his wife has given up and told him to curse God and die, he replies that even if God should choose to take his life, he would still choose to love and serve Him. These are not idle words; Job speaks from experience. Job was a man rich in material things—land, animals, servants and a large, loving family. And not only was he wealthy by the world's standards, but he was wealthy in light of God's economy as well. He was a man who loved and revered God and had taught his children to live for God. Before he started each day, he spent time talking with God, and lived righteously before the world. That love relationship was reciprocal; God also loved Job and held him in high esteem.

One day when God and Satan were talking, God used Job as an example of one who loved and revered Him. And Satan replied something to the effect that, "Of course Job loves You! Why shouldn't he? You've given him everything his heart desires. I'll bet if you strip him of everything he holds dear, he will curse You to Your face." And God gave Satan permission to test him, with one condition. He would not be allowed to cause him personal injury or take his life.

Following is the scriptural account of what happened next:

> One day when Job's sons and daughters were feasting and drinking wine at the oldest brother's house, a messenger came to Job and said, "The oxen were plowing and the donkeys were grazing nearby, and the Sabeans attacked and carried them all off. They put the servants to the sword, and I am the only one who has escaped to tell you!
>
> While he was yet speaking, another messenger came and said, "The fire of God fell from the sky and burned up the sheep and the servants, and I am the only one who has escaped to tell you!
>
> While he was still speaking, another messenger came and said, "The Caldeans formed three raiding parties and swept down on your camels and carried them off. They put the servants to the sword, and I am the only one who has escaped to tell you!
>
> While he was still speaking, yet another messenger came and said, "Your sons and daughters were feasting and drinking wine at the oldest brother's house , when suddenly a mighty wind swept in from the desert and struck the four corners of the house. It collapsed on them and they are all dead, and I am the only one who has escaped to tell you!"
>
> (Job 1:12-19 NIV)

He had lost virtually everything. Of all the possible broken world experiences, this has to be the worst.

Job, a humble man, wasn't bitter about the experience. Instead he responded quietly, "Naked came I from my mother's womb, and naked shall I return... The Lord gave and the Lord hath taken away. Blessed be the name of the Lord" (Job 1:21 NIV).

Later God spoke again to Satan, this time, asking if he had as yet broken Job's spirit. God already knew the answer, but wanted Satan to admit he had lost the challenge. This time, Satan answered that Job would curse God to His face if he were allowed to injure his body. Once again God gave Satan permission to wound Job, this time physically. Satan caused Job to break out in boils all over his body. There was no comfort or relief from the pain and misery he endured during this time. And to top it all off, several friends, who were also very religious men, came to supposedly comfort him.

In their collective diatribe, these three men accused him of hidden sin, telling him that if he would only repent, the curse would be lifted. Not long after that, when Job finally lost his will to live, God visited him in person. He showed Job His greatness, His power and His sovereignty. In the end He asked Job a question. He wanted to know where Job was when He created the universe.

Job answered, "I know that You can do all things; no plan of yours can be thwarted. You asked, 'Who is this that obscures my counsel without knowledge?' Surely I spoke things I did not understand, things too wonderful for me to know. You said, 'Listen now and I will speak; I will question you, and you shall answer me.' My ears had heard of You but now my eyes have seen You. Therefore I despise myself and repent in dust and ashes" (Job 42:1-6 NIV).

I do so enjoy happy endings, and this story of a broken world does have a happy ending. In obedience to God, Job, with uncommon kindness, chose to pray for his miserable comforters, and the Lord turned the situation around and blessed Job abundantly. Scripture says, "The Lord blessed the latter part of Job's life more than the first" (Job 42:12 NIV).

Job and his wife had more sons and daughters and were able to see them grow up and flourish to the fourth generation. His faith in God was rewarded with great blessing.

CHAPTER ELEVEN

David

I love to read. And as strange as it may seem, I went through a period in my life where all I wanted to do was read romance novels. I was reading two or three a week by the time the Holy Spirit convicted me, and it was only then that I realized why they so attracted me. He showed me that I was identifying with the macho images of the heroes in the stories.

In a personal revelation, He told me that His love letters to me in scripture were much more enriching than all the romances I could ever read.

It wasn't long after this when I discovered the story of the life of David, and I haven't read a romance novel since.

To know David is to love him. God even called him the apple of His eye. One reason David's story so intrigues me is that his is the story of every man. Though he was human and made many painful choices and costly mistakes, God loved him through it all. He chose to exalt him, simply because his heart was tender. And no matter how much trouble he got into, when the spirit convicted him, he repented and quickly turned his life around, once again walking in righteousness.

David's life, as detailed in scripture, was full of trials, inflicting painful and repeated wounds, and yet each time a new trial came, he chose to seek God, and ultimately became intimate with a God merciful enough to forgive and yet strong enough to restore.

During the reign of Saul, God exalted him to a place of greatness, and where once he had once walked in faith toward God, he, over time, began to believe his own press releases, and became proud and cocky. Because of that, God judged him and told him he would remove him as king and replace him with someone else.

Samuel, the priest at the time, loved Saul and was nearly ill with grief over his loss of the throne. But God spoke to Samuel and said, "How long will you mourn for Saul, since I have rejected him as king over Israel? Fill your horn with oil and be on your way; I am sending you to Jesse of Bethlehem. I have chosen one of his sons to be king" (1 Samuel 16:1 NIV). Samuel arrived and saw seven of Jesse's sons and asked if there were any more, after God did not choose any of the seven sons. As the youngest of Jesse's eight sons, David was probably in his early teens at the time, and it appears that no one thought he would be chosen, since he wasn't even in the lineup when Samuel arrived. When young David was finally brought before Samuel, the Lord said, "Rise up and anoint him; he is the one. So Samuel took the horn of oil and anointed him in the presence of his brothers, and from that day on the Spirit of the Lord came upon David in power" (1 Samuel 16:12-13 NIV).

About that time, the spirit of the Lord departed from Saul, leaving him open to torment from an evil spirit, constantly restless and upset. After examining their options, his attendants suggested hiring someone to come and play the harp to calm his nerves. And not coincidentally, Saul's assistant remembered seeing David play the harp and thought he might be just the one for the job. Shortly David was brought before the king and played for him. Saul evidently felt some kind of relief and was pleased enough with the young man that he hired him into part time service as a harpist. Over time, David and Saul grew to be close friends and allies, but it wouldn't last.

Because David had spent long periods of time as a shepherd, guarding his father's sheep, he had become a crack shot with a simple slingshot and stones. In fact, scripture says he killed both a bear and a lion while he was still just a boy. At one point, David saw Saul and his armies cowering when faced by the Philistine army. One soldier, in particular, provoked David to anger with his derogatory remarks about the God of Israel.

When David saw that Saul and his armies were too afraid to confront the giant man, David did what he could with the skills he had. He put a stone in his slingshot, called out the giant Goliath, and killed him with one flick of his wrist, believing that God would defeat the enemy. At that point,

Saul gave David more responsibility and eventually put him in charge of part of his army. But all was not well between the David and Saul.

By now, David was becoming well known and highly esteemed for his physical prowess and mighty deeds, so much so that the people, within Saul's hearing, praised David's deeds over Saul's. As you might imagine, Saul was fit to be tied. And from that time on, Saul felt threatened and did everything in his power to supplant David's rise to power, including hatching a scheme to kill him. After failing several times to kill David, Saul assigned him to the battlefront, hoping he would die, but God had other plans and stationed angels around him to preserve his life.

From the Palace to a Cave

David had to run to stay one step ahead of Saul's death plot. Harassed and pursued, he was, using our metaphor, shot and wounded by someone close to him, then shot again while he was down. By now, King Saul was not just losing his kingdom, but his sanity as well, and took 3,000 men out to kill David and anyone who tried to protect him. The only safe place for David to hide was in caves (1 Samuel 24:1, 2). One night, Saul went into a cave to sleep, unaware that David and his small band of loyal friends were already deep in the same cave. At any moment, David could have killed Saul and ended his own suffering, but even with a wounded spirit, David thought it over and decided such behavior would not be pleasing to God. In the end, David spared Saul's life, but crept close enough to cut off a piece of his robe 1 Samuel 24:10). David's conscience condemned him for even that. He simply could not in good conscience lift his hand against God's anointed. Twice in a very short span of time, David had opportunities to kill Saul and end the harassment. David chose not to usurp God's sovereignty, but instead left the situation up to Him.

Unjustly persecuted, David had to be emotionally shattered by all that was happening, and yet he never lost hope in the Lord. The book of Psalms repeatedly shows David crying out to God to vindicate him. As if David wasn't under enough pressure by then, at the same time he and his men were fighting a winning battle with the Philistines, the enemy raided their town, burning their homes and kidnapping their wives and children. Not surprisingly, David and his men were devastated, unable to imagine how such a thing could have happened.

Tragically, David's men, his warriors, his 'brothers in the faith' did not handle their grief well, and because they needed someone to blame, they pointed the finger at David, and even discussed whether or not to stone him. David must have been dumbfounded. His remnant of supporters had now turned against him, and he had to feel abandoned and isolated as never before. In their grief, these dear friends became his worst enemies, as in Matthew 10:36, where it speaks of "a man's enemies being those of his own household." At this point, David had a decision to make. He could either let despair get the best of him or choose to draw near to God for comfort.

The interesting thing here is that David had lots of practice drawing near to God during times of trial. The Lord had met the challenge every time, building David's faith. So as was his habit, he began to review all the ways God had run to his aid, and in the process, scripture says he comforted himself. At that moment God reminded David that He was still in control and able to turn around for good what the enemy meant for harm. God told him to rise up, go after the enemy and He would, without fail, restore all that David had lost. And He did exactly that, for both David and those of his brethren who had been devastated.

You and I are not immune to the ups and downs of life, and will, if we live long enough, experience grief, disappointments and rejections, but the deepest pain is often felt at the betrayal by those closest to us.

How are we to respond to these times of heartache? What are we to do?

Just like David, we need to draw near to God and review in our hearts all the ways He has proved his faithfulness. In so doing, we will comfort ourselves, shoring up our spirits to keep going—not letting these injuries develop into a wounded spirit, which could, at some point, be the death-blow to our faith.

Another lesson we can learn from David relates to the consequences of sin. David, in spite of his heart toward God and all his mighty exploits, wasn't able to reign in his lusts. And in fact, he lusted after and eventually seduced another man's wife. To complicate things further, her husband was one of David's highest-ranking 'mighty men of valor'. David's sin of adultery immediately followed one of his greatest victories, when he fought and won over the Ammonite-Syrians. Seven hundred chariots were destroyed, forty thousand horsemen were killed, and all the kings allied to the Ammonites and Syrians fled, leaving all the people to serve Israel (see 2 Samuel 10:19).

When Bathsheba became pregnant, David knew he was in deep trouble. Desperate to cover up his sinful behavior, he had to try to salvage his reputation by heading off what he knew would be a terrible scandal. He thought he had come up with the perfect plan when he had her husband sent home from the battle for a supposed war council at the palace, but Uriah saw through the pretense and asked what was going on. David bluffed his way through the visit and told him to go home to his wife for the night, but Uriah refused, saying that in all good conscience, he couldn't return to the comfort of his home while leaving his comrades in the heat of battle. When David's plan backfired and Uriah returned to the battle, David felt he had no choice but to order him to the front lines, where he was, predictably, killed. As soon as he could arrange it, David took Bathsheba as his wife, and for a year, things went fairly well, if you overlook the guilt that must have been haunting David's thoughts both day and night.

One day, Nathan, the prophet of the Lord and a loving friend of David's, came and told him a story. He told how a poor man had a little lamb that he loved, that was part of his family, and how a rich man with huge flocks and herds made plans to entertain guests. Because he didn't want to kill any of his sheep for the meal, he ordered his servant to steal and kill the poor man's sheep, which he then had prepared for his guests.

When David heard the story, he was furious and announced that the rich man should be killed for doing such a terrible thing. Nathan, heartbroken at having to confront his friend, said, "You are the man. You have despised the commandments of the Lord" (2 Samuel 12:1-9 NIV), adding that he had done it in secret and would now pay the consequences of his sin.

David, stricken by the truth of his sin, fell to his face before Nathan and repented of his sin. After a word from the Lord, Nathan said that David was forgiven and would not die, "but..." If only things could have gone back to normal with no price to pay, but it was not to be. The child born to Bathsheba would die, and the sword would never leave David's house.

For the rest of David's life, there was enmity in his home, and before it was over, he was estranged from his sons, three of whom were lost in battle. He paid the price of sin with heartache after heartache, only confirming Nathan's prophecy regarding the consequences of sin.

Don't be fooled. There are always consequences for sin. This was true for Adam and Eve. It was true for David, and it is true for you and me. Sin may look irresistible, and may even look like the right thing to do. But sin is a lie, and it is out to trick you the same way Satan tricked Eve.

If you read an erotic magazine with a nude centerfold, you are playing with fire.

Here is what Major Ian Thomas says regarding the mind:

What is it that preoccupies your imagination as a redeemed sinner? With what does your mind busy itself? What are your ambitions? What are your appetites? Where do you go, what company do you keep and what do you do—in your mind?

Sin is conceived in the imagination. First there comes the suggestion—the satanic suggestion—and that suggestion becomes a desire; and if it is allowed to conceive and mature and be brought to birth within the area of your imagination, the desire will become an intent that you have already sinned, whether your circumstances allow you to implement your intent or not. That is why the Lord Jesus Christ said: 'Whosoever looketh on a woman to lust after her hath committed adultery with her already in his heart' (Matthew 5:28).

Where suggestion becomes desire, desire becomes intent, and intent becomes an act. An act becomes a memory and that memory is hung like a picture upon the wall of your imagination, in the picture gallery of your mind. When later in your thoughts you wander through the picture gallery, you see the memory on the wall, and this memory itself becomes a suggestion, and this suggestion becomes desire, and this desire becomes intent, and if this desire becomes an act, you will have hanging on the wall two memories, and the process can begin all over again with double force.

Do you see the principle? That is why every time you commit another sin, you make it easier to commit another sin, because every time you commit a sin, you are making "an altar to sin" (Hosea 8:11a). Every sinful memory stimulates sinful desire, encourages sinful intent, and another sinful act which will become yet another sinful memory, until your mind is polluted."[6]

David was the apple of God's eye, but he still fell into sin, by an act of his own will. He repented, and God forgave him, but he continued to pay the consequences of that sin for the rest of his life.

CHAPTER TWELVE

Jonah

Have you ever been through a spiritual dry spell? There are times in every Christian's life that he experiences no divine presence. In these times we have no yearning to read God's Word; we do read the Bible and pray, but only out of obligation. When I feel this way, I often wonder if God is hearing my prayers or if I'm talking to myself.

Jonah was going through a dry spell, after clearly hearing from God on many occasions. Even though he may have continued to read the Word and to pray, He hadn't heard from God or felt His presence in a very long time.

Finally God broke the silence and spoke to Jonah, telling him to go to Ninevah and preach the gospel.

Because he was so unaccustomed to hearing God's voice, he may have doubted that it was God speaking. Or he may have been angry, bitter because of God's long period of silence, but in either case, he turned away from Ninevah and rushed in the opposite direction.

In his book, *Rebuilding Your Broken World*, author Gordon MacDonald addressed Jonah's predicament this way:

THE BROKEN WORLD OF JONAH

"Centuries later another man, now quite famous, saw his world fall apart in a rather unique fashion. If Moses ended up deep in a desert when his world broke, Jonah the prophet ended up deep in the sea, and it is likely that he thought he would never see land again. Again, my imagination attempts to penetrate some of Jonah's more difficult moments, wondering just what he was thinking.

Reporter: Mr. Jonah? Sir, I am from the *Jerusalem Post.*

Jonah: How in the world did you guys find me here?

Reporter: Little bit of luck, really. We got word that you'd gone overboard in the storm last week, and when the search was called off, we printed your obituary. Then someone up here saw your picture with the obit and called and said that you were staying at the inn.

Jonah: So everyone down there thinks I'm dead? Well, I suppose I might as well be dead for all that happened.

Reporter: We'd like to help clear up that little misunderstanding by telling your story. I mean, this is some distance from Joppa. So someone must have brought you up here.

Jonah: Um...Actually, I came by whale.

Reporter: Right. Say, could you go into that a bit? I mean it is a little hard to swallow.

Jonah: Look, years ago I made a commitment to the God of Israel that I'd live in total obedience to His purposes—that I'd go anywhere, say anything and do it at any cost to proclaim the truth of God.

Reporter: Okay. So what does that have to do with the whale?

Jonah: I'm coming to that. You've just got to understand that when God said, 'Go to Nineveh,' I...

Reporter: Did you say Nineveh?

Jonah: That was my reaction too. Nineveh? I mean, I haven't made it a habit of questioning God before, but I certainly did then. I protested with everything in me against going.

Reporter: What were you supposed to do in Nineveh?

Jonah: What does a prophet of the Lord do? Preach, of course.

Reporter: Preach what?

Jonah: Repentance. Tell them God would judge the city unless they all repented.

Reporter: How does that link up with going overboard in a storm? Could you get to the whale?

Jonah: Frankly, I decided that I wasn't going to Nineveh—that God was going to have to find some other idiot to go there. I guess you could say I resigned from the priesthood.

Reporter: And the storm?

Jonah: Well, maybe I should rephrase that. You don't really resign from prophethood exactly. You run, and I ran for Joppa and found the ship that was sailing very soon in the opposite direction.

Reporter: And it sailed into a storm.

Jonah: In more ways than one. Those guys thought they had a storm going. I had one far larger inside me.

Reporter: Inside you?

Jonah: You make a bad choice, like the one I did, and you suffer for it. I walked around in a daze, angry with myself, full of self-doubt and fear. Here I was, leaving everything that was important to me, running to a city I'd never even seen before. I was furious at God for forcing me into something I didn't want to do. In effect, I'd dug in my heels and said no.

Reporter: Did it work?

Jonah: It worked until the storm broke out inside me. I was in such denial that I'd gone to sleep down in the ship after it left port. I found that I could sleep almost around the clock, even through the storm, until the captain woke me and seemed to think that I knew the cause of the storm. He also said he'd appreciate my praying for the men on deck. Of course, he was right. I did know something about the storm.

Reporter: So what did you know?

Jonah: That the storm outside was merely an extension of the storm inside me. In other words, I was the cause of the storm. So I had them throw me overboard.

Reporter: They threw you overboard?

Jonah: I made them do it. I felt so cheap and worthless. My sin of rebellion and disobedience was hurting other people. They were about to die in the storm that I had created, and they were terrified.

I had no recourse, but to force them to throw me over, and when they did, the winds and rain ceased immediately.

Reporter: What about for you?

Jonah: You could say that the storm lasted three more days as God let me live inside a whale and think about whether or not I still wanted to live in rebellion. In essence, he put me in a tight place without any distractions, forcing me to face a hard choice—whether I wanted to go on this way or turn around and go in God's direction?

Reporter: And what did you decide?

Jonah: I'm here, aren't I?

Reporter: So what happens next, Mr. Jonah?

Jonah: You see that road over there? It leads to Nineveh.[7]

When I was running from God, I told people that I was a modern day Jonah. Though I personally was not swallowed by a big fish, I was swallowed by what is called the Faith movement, or name-it-and-claim-it heresy. Because I really wanted to get rich, I fooled myself into believing that if I couldn't preach anymore, I could support preachers and missionaries from my wealth.

My fish could also be called MLM (Multi Level Marketing), for me it turned out to be Much Loved Money! The first fish or MLM was, believe it or not, a get-rich-quick scheme. If I gave $200.00 and had two other people who would have two other people give $200.00, eventually I'd be a millionaire if all went according to plan. Well, guess what? The man who presented this grand opportunity took all the money and ran.

I was spewed out of the fish's belly onto dry land, having lost a great deal of money. But did I learn my lesson? No, in fact, I turned around and did it again and again. Each time swallowed by a different MLM, but together, they swallowed up my entire investment. Scripture says the love of money is the root of all kinds of evil. Some, eager for money, have wandered from the faith and pierced themselves with much grief. (1 Timothy 6:10)

A son in the Lord felt compassion for me and knew I was not living right, so he proposed that I work for his ministry, called Market Place Ministries. I blew off the opportunity, looking to make my fortune. But, like Jonah, I was only running from God.

If I was God and had a child who acted like me, I would have turned around in disgust and walked away, but God is faithful. He never left me, though I had more use for money than for Him at the time.

Today when I hear the words 'MLM' I imagine a giant sucker fish with his mouth open, ready to swallow up any fool that even gets close.

CHAPTER THIRTEEN

Peter

The young Jewish boy would have learned the Tora/torah, the Talmud, and would have read the Midrash before he became a man at 13 years of age. The parents referred to them as learning the Letters.

Tora/torah=

1. a) Learning law, instruction, etc. b) [usually T-] the whole body of Jewish literature, including the Scripture and the Talmud.
2. [usually T-] a) the Pentateuch b) pl. to rot or torot a parchment scroll containing the Pentateuch

Talmud = the collection of writings constituting the Jewish and religious law. It consists of two parts: The Mishna (text) and Gemara (commentary), but the term is sometimes restricted to the Gemara.

Midrash = Judaism any of the rabbinical commentaries and explanatory notes on the Scriptures, written between the beginning of exile and c. AD.

IMPULSIVE PETER

"Sometimes you try my patience to the hilt, boy," said John.

"But Poppa, I really did see a huge fish on the other side of the boat," said Simon, as he stretched his arms wide to show his father the size of the fish.

"Which way is the wind blowing? Which is the leeward side? We lost a net because you lowered them on the wrong side. You'd better start thinking. If you insist on doing things your way on impulse, you'll have to stay home with your momma. You hear me, boy?" said Poppa, his voice getting louder with every word.

"Yes, Poppa."

A big boy for twelve years old, Simon was already nearly as tall as his father. He had developed a deep tan and thick, muscular arms, after long days of hauling nets in the sunshine.

When the nets brought in plenty of fish, Simon loved to sort the good fish from the bad, setting the good ones in one place, while the rejects, along with the crabs, were thrown overboard.

He hated cleaning the fish, but he was good at it, able to keep up with the most experienced men. Sometimes, when he cleaned the catch, Poppa would yell, "Simon, don't eat all the fish eggs. Save some for the market. You're eating up all the profits."

They always kept an eye on him, after catching him in the act of tossing the good catch overboard, so he wouldn't have to clean it. That's the way he was, acting on the spur of the moment, impulsive, without thought for the consequences. When asked why he did these kinds of things, he had no answer.

Simon had been going out on the boat with his father ever since he was big enough to walk. He loved the water, sailing, and fishing. On days the boat did not go out, Simon went to the synagogue to study the Torah. He was twelve now, and in one year he would have his bar mitzvah, signifying to the world that he was a man.

Simon loved studying the Torah, but sometimes he questioned his father as to why he had to study and learn letters when he was going to become a fisherman. "I could see it, if I were going to be a rabbi," he mused aloud.

John answered his son, "Simon, two things come to you as you study the Torah. First is the writing of the letters and secondly is learning to know the author of the Torah in a personal way."

Simon shrugged. "Well, all right, but I'll never be a writer of letters, and it's obvious that the author of the Torah has forgotten me." After a pause, he sighed. "All right. I'll learn it for you, but when I'm old enough, I'll put all of this away. When I am grown up and have my own boat, I'll do what I want."

His father looked at him with sad eyes. "That's all I can ask. Just obey me now, and I will be able to say that I did the best that I could do. But, one thing I ask, Simon... You often act before you think. Please be diligent and listen while rabbi is teaching. Put your whole heart into learning the letters and the Torah, and I'll pray that Yahweh will come to you in a personal way. I love you, Simon."

Simon put his head down and said very softly, "I love you too, Poppa."

The impact of his father's message was written on Simon's heart, even though he tried to shake it off. And over the years, he grew in stature and mastered both his letters and the Torah.

The fishing haul was good most of the time, and before long, he was running his own boat alongside that of his brother, Andrew. They would take their boats out early every morning and come back late just before sundown. They hand picked their help and trained them well, so that if the brothers needed time off, their excellent crews could manage without them.

One day, they saw that large crowds had gathered and were listening to a strange looking man. Word was that this man came down from the mountains and was preaching and baptizing people in the Jordan River. Simon said to his brother, "This should be fun. Come on. Let's go." Andrew agreed, so they left their boats to the men they had trained and went to hear what the man was preaching.

He was indeed a strange man; dressed unlike anyone they had ever seen, wearing only a loincloth. His beard was dripping with honey and had locust wings tangled in it, but his words made people forget his appearance. He asked the people why they came to hear him speak, but before anyone could answer, he told them they were lacking something in their spiritual lives. He told them that they were sinners and needed to repent and be baptized for the remission of their sins. Boldly, he proclaimed, "There is One coming, called the Lamb of God, who will take away all your sins." When people asked, John answered that he himself was not the Messiah, but came to prepare the way for Him.

Simon and Andrew left the crowd and neither said a word as they walked home, deep in thought after what they had just heard. The next morning Simon said to Andrew, "You know, I think I'd like to spend a little more time with his followers, so I can hear more of what he has to say." Andrew felt the same way. Together they became dedicated followers of John the Baptist, interested in learning about the coming Messiah.

One day while John the Baptist was preaching and baptizing, he stopped and was very quiet, thoughtfully considering a man who stood on the riverbank. John pointed to Him and said, "Behold the Lamb of God who takes away the sin of the world!"

Amazing them all, the stranger walked into the water and asked to be baptized. Looking chagrined, John bowed and said, "Lord, I'm not worthy to tie your shoes. You should be baptizing me." But Jesus disagreed, asking John to baptize him to signify the beginning of his public ministry, so John did as He asked. While John was still baptizing Jesus, the heavens opened, and the Holy Spirit descended upon Him in a form of a dove, accompanied by a voice from heaven, saying, "Thou art my beloved Son; in thee I am well pleased" (Luke 3:22).

Simon and Andrew heard the voice and fell to their knees in awe, well aware that no man could see God and live. They instinctively recognized the voice of Yahweh, and it left them trembling violently.

Jesus walked out of the water and everyone watched as he walked away, until finally Simon and Andrew rose and walked slowly back to their boats. As they were parting, Simon said, "You go back tomorrow and see if this man Jesus comes again." Andrew just nodded in affirmation, still too choked up by what he had seen to utter a single word.

The next morning, bright and early, Andrew went to the river where John preached and baptized. He got there before John and as the crowd waited, he heard others mention wishing to see Jesus again. Though he couldn't put his finger on what it was, there was just something about Him... Some said that He was the long awaited Messiah, but others argued that He was just another Jew who wanted to be baptized for the remission of sins. No one could be sure of anything yet, but there was endless speculation.

Before long, Andrew was drawn into conversation with others interested in Jesus, and he excitedly told how he had heard the voice of Yahweh and seen a dove from heaven come to rest on Jesus' shoulder. The people around him shook their heads and backed away, looking at him as if he was crazy, but Andrew didn't care. He knew what he had seen, and this kind of thing just did not happen everyday.

Finally John came and preached to the people who were, by now, quite a large crowd.

Everyone was looking for this man Jesus, but He didn't appear that day or even the next. In fact, it was nearly fifty days later before anyone ever saw Him again. When Simon asked Andrew for news of Him, Andrew told him that no one knew where Jesus went. During this time, John continued preaching and baptizing, repeatedly saying that Messiah would come, but would baptize, not with water, but with the Holy Ghost.

One day while John was baptizing people in the Jordan River there was a commotion on the bank, and John stopped and looked up. Someone yelled, "He's here, the One you baptized." John said, "Yes, this is the Messiah, the One whom God sent." Jesus didn't speak, but merely acknowledged John with a nod of His head and turned again to leave.

Mesmerized by the man for reasons they didn't understand, Andrew and the one who was with him followed Jesus, and when they had gone away from the crowd, Jesus turned to them and asked them what they wanted. Andrew asked, "Where are you staying, sir?"

Jesus gestured to them. "Come and see."

When Andrew and his friend were invited to spend the day with Jesus, Andrew hurried away to find Simon. On the way back, he could barely contain his excitement when he said this was the Messiah for whom they had been waiting.

Jesus saw them coming and went to meet them. When he saw Simon, he said, "You are Simon, son of John, you shall be called *Petros*." Simon knew from his time in the classroom that the name Peter meant "a chip off the rock".

This impulsive man right then and there became a follower of Jesus, and just as he had learned to listen to the rabbi, he now learned to listen and think about what this man Jesus was saying. Even though his name was changed, he was still the same old impulsive Simon, whose independent spirit was strong-willed and stubborn.

One night when Jesus came to the disciples' boat, in the middle of a storm, He walked on the water. Peter saw him, jumped overboard and began walking toward Jesus. When he realized what he was doing, he took his eyes off of Jesus, and began to sink as he cried, "Save me!" Jesus reached out and hauled him out of the water and together they returned to the boat.

After listening to His teaching, Peter grew to admire Jesus, and soon became a member of Jesus' inner circle, along with James and John.

The next three years passed quickly, and once again Passover time drew near. As they were preparing to eat the Seder or Passover Feast, Jesus began to wash the disciples' feet. When he came to Peter, Peter frowned and shook his head. "Lord, don't stoop so low as to wash my feet."

Jesus told him that if he didn't let Him wash his feet he would have no part of His life. At that, Peter replied, "Then give me a whole bath." Jesus smiled. "Washing your feet is enough. You don't understand what I am doing yet, but you will when you begin to minister for me." Jesus was speaking of the humility that would be required for their future teaching ministries.

While eating the Passover Feast, Jesus told them that he was going to be killed. Without thinking, Peter responded to Jesus and told Him that he would die with Him if need be. Meeting his gaze, Jesus told him, "Before the rooster crows, you will deny me three times."

Peter said "Not me, Lord".

After the feast, Jesus took the disciples to the Mount of Olives, but left them and went farther in the garden to pray alone, apparently very upset. In fact, He prayed for such a long time that the weary disciples finally succumbed to sleep. This happened three times, and each time, Jesus went back, woke them up and told them to pray with Him. Finally, He told them to get up because soldiers were coming for him.

When the crowd got to where they were, Peter pulled out his sword and cut off the right ear of the servant of the high priest. Jesus rebuked Peter, picked up the man's ear and healed him.

With no apparent cause, the soldiers arrested Jesus and hustled Him to the High Priest's palace, where they made arrangements for a last minute trial.

The house had an outer and an inner court and a person had to know the host to get into the inner court. Peter was in the outer court and a young girl asked him if he knew Jesus. Peter vehemently denied any knowledge of Him, and when, only a short time later, two others asked if he was a follower of Jesus, he angrily denied that he knew Jesus. As he was swearing and cursing, the rooster crowed and Jesus met Peter's troubled gaze, giving him a look that spoke more loudly than words ever could have.

It reminded him of Jesus' warning, "Before the rooster crows, you will deny me three times." Jesus' look broke his heart. That single incident was a turning point of his life, as he repented, wept bitterly over his sin, and went from there transformed.

We see that even though Peter's nature was impulsive and his wound self-inflicted, the Holy Spirit was able to change him when he repented. God used him mightily after this. This man changed from being impulsive to impeccable because he allowed the Holy Spirit to heal his broken heart.

CHAPTER FOURTEEN

The Apostle Paul

Very little is actually known about the early life of the Apostle Paul, whose name was originally Saul of Tarsus. According to the historical record, written by Jerome, both of his parents came from Gischala in Galilee. His father was of the tribe of Benjamin, a full-blooded Jew on both his mother's and his father's sides of the family.

There is reason to believe Saul may have lost his mother at a young age, though scripture doesn't specifically mention it. In any case, his father would have been responsible for his education, and clearly, Saul's family had high hopes for his future. Apparently his father was a man of means, able to give him the best education money could buy, allowing Saul to learn first in what we would call a Jewish kindergarten, and later from those high in authority in the synagogue, men of social and political influence. Saul had always had an enquiring mind, and although he was quite learned by the time he reached adulthood, he apparently still had many questions, all of which were answered the very instant he later met Jesus. It's interesting to note that although he was highly educated, he lived the life of a laborer, having come from a family of tanners, merchants who owned and worked in a leather-tanning factory, where the hair of Sicilian goats was woven into what is known as 'cilicium textiles'. Working with the coarse hair was tough on the hands, so we know Saul was not unfamiliar with hard work. Scripture further explains that as an adult and an itinerant preacher, Paul supported himself by making tents. It would not be surprising if, as a child,

Saul had accompanied his father on business trips and to the nearby harbor, where they had access to the latest news of the outside world.

During Saul's later years as a student, the focus of his education began to change. Where he was taught basic church history as a young child, later on the teachers introduced him to the concept of what is referred to as 'the fence of the law' and the numerous Old Testament purification rites, purportedly required to keep one in right relationship with God. This had to be a heavy load on the sensitive young man's spirit, since he was very bright and easily taught. He knew that the law, though harsh, was good, when used lawfully, according to 1 Timothy 1:8, and yet, on the other hand, heard the Pharisees encouraging students to use rational solutions as well as the voice of reason when dealing with the law. Clearly he saw this as compromise.

These two opposing points of view may have caused Saul confusion and opened a gaping chasm, a credibility gap in his mind. It is hinted there may have even been times of humiliation, when he tried to bring up and justify the two opposing scenarios in his mind. He says in Romans 7:10 that what "was intended to bring life actually brought death." After completing his Jewish education, he chose not to marry, but to continue what we might call his 'secular' education, which included Greek philosophy and mastery of the Greek language, which allowed pupils to later keep in touch with provincial governors. Most Jewish teachers of that day, feeling it was beneath them, strictly shunned the idea of learning anything having to do with Greece. By today's standards, Paul could easily have boasted of having had a PhD in Jewish Law and another in Greek philosophy. Because Paul's excellent educational opportunities placed him in line for positions of authority in government and politics, they also offered opportunity for pride.

Let's follow Paul's life and see why God had His hand on him the way He did. In our examination of his life, we will see why God chose to use him in such an amazing way. Paul was still a young man when accepted into the Sanhedrin. His standing with this group of religious Jews gave him authority to seek out and prosecute a new sect of people who believed a new and strange doctrine. They taught that Messiah had already come in the person of Jesus Christ of Nazareth. These people claimed to be Jews, but were no longer accepted by the Orthodox Jews of their day, and it was Paul's esteemed assignment to put a stop to such terrible heresy. He excelled at his task, putting at risk of death everyone who even whispered such sacrilege. Stephen is the only one mentioned by name whom Paul harmed, and in his case, he held Stephen's coat while others stoned him to death.

God allowed this heartbreaking activity to go on, but only for a time, before grabbing Paul's attention in a very unusual way. Paul, on horseback, was headed to the city of Damascus, when God appeared to him in a dazzlingly bright light. Frightened by the light, the horse shied, flinging Paul to the ground. During this incident, Paul was struck blind, and heard a loud voice say, "Saul, Saul, why do you persecute me?"

"Who are you, Lord?" asked Saul.

"I am Jesus, whom you are persecuting. Now get up and go..." (Acts 9:4,5).

The Lord said of Paul in verse fifteen, "This is my chosen instrument to carry my name before the Gentiles and their kings and before the people of Israel. *I will show him how he must suffer for my name*" (Acts 9:15,16). (Emphasis mine.)

Paul never gave less than 100 percent of himself to whatever cause he espoused, both before and after his conversion experience. In fact, we hold him up as an example of successful Christian leadership. But what is it that made Paul such a success? How was he able to live so far above the circumstances, so dedicated to Jesus Christ? It is clear from his teachings that Paul was totally convinced that Jesus was God's Son, that judgment was coming, and that God had forgiven his sins because of the blood of Jesus. His letters emphasize these truths at least as much as did his life.

Paul believed, without a doubt, that judgment was imminent, and he was ready to face that judgment, not through his own righteous deeds or his excellent understanding of God's thoughts and intentions, but because of the blood of Jesus that had completely and forever covered his sins, restoring him to right relationship to God (Philippians 3:9). Because of his firm belief in the coming judgment, Paul sought to obey God in all things and especially in regard to warning others of this judgment. And because he understood that his righteousness was because of Jesus, he was at the same time gentle and firm in his relationships with others, and yet gratefully confident in his own identity in Christ. As much as we might like to believe it, Paul was no Superman. He was very human, but was also totally sincere and committed to his task of preaching the message of salvation to a fallen world.

In the course of his Christian experience, he went through myriad difficult situations. These words describe his life.

> I have worked much harder, been in prison more frequently, been flogged more severely, and been exposed to death again and again. Five times I received from the Jews the forty lashes minus one. Three times I was beaten with rods, once I was stoned, three times I was shipwrecked, I spent a night and a day in the open sea...I have been in danger from rivers, in danger of bandits, in danger in the country, in danger at sea, and in danger from false brothers.
>
> I have labored and toiled and have often gone without sleep; I have known hunger and thirst and have often gone without food; I have been cold and naked. Besides everything else, I face daily the pressure of my concern for all the churches.
>
> (2 Corinthians 11:23-28 NIV)

Paul endured all this and at the same time struggled with something he referred to as a 'thorn in the flesh'. What is the nature of this thorn? Many have sought to define it. Some have suggested malaria, others epilepsy, and yet others, some sort of eye ailment. Perhaps God purposely left this issue vague, simply so we could identify with Paul's struggles.

It fascinates me to observe how little Paul was esteemed by other Christians of his day. In spite of his many amazing gifts, his unceasing labors, and God's clear blessing on his ministry, he put up with a neverending stream of criticism. And in fact, the Corinthian people were especially vehement in their scorn, accusing him of levity and vacillation, questioning his motives for everything. They even spread the word that he was unreliable and contradicted his own words. In 2 Corinthians 12, we see Paul beginning a new phase with regard to answering these charges. As amazing as it sounds, he was, at that point, caught up into paradise while in a vision, where he was shown things so awesome that he simply couldn't explain or repeat them. This reminds us that revelation, as far as we're concerned, is incomplete. God knows more of His glory than He feels is necessary to reveal to man.

Paul experienced what most of us only dream of. And although it may have occurred to him to boast about what had happened, the aforementioned thorn in the flesh apparently kept him otherwise preoccupied. Being human, Paul must have thought he would be much more effective in his service to the Lord without the constant struggle with the thorn, and yet God chose not to remove it, even after he prayed. From scripture, we know that the thorn was given "lest I should be exalted above measure through the abundance of the revelations" (12:7 kjv). As we can clearly see, God blessed and anointed Paul for ministry, but in order to remain useful to God, he had to be free of pride. The same danger exists for those of us who are blessed and anointed for the work of the gospel. Because we are so abundantly blessed, it is often easy to forget that we have nothing but what we have received from the Lord.

How then did Paul react after praying three times for the thorn to be removed and hearing God answer 'No'? Certainly, from scripture, we see that the thorn hindered him in some way, and he felt desperate that it be removed. At times, we may become angry and disappointed with ourselves for less than stellar behavior when confronted with trials, but we can comfort ourselves, remembering that even the Apostle Paul sometimes struggled against God's will. In fact, God knows believers must walk through struggles in order to process feelings and finally come to a place of acceptance.

Often, God's will seems utterly overwhelming, as we so clearly see from Jesus' experience in Gethsemane. The plan the Father had for him was stupefying in its horror (Mark 4:33). So much so, that he wept, praying that it be removed. Though there may be little resemblance between our struggles and those of the Lord Jesus, it gives us hope to realize that God doesn't expect us to simply accept His will without flinching. More often than not, it takes a process of grieving and tears to finally come to a place of complete acceptance of God's will.

How does the Lord answer Paul's prayer? "My grace is sufficient for you, for my power is made perfect in weakness" (v. 9). Though God heard, He did not choose to say yes. The thorn would not be removed, and not only that, but the thorn required Paul to depend on the Lord and not on himself to persevere and be victorious in spite of it. The lesson we learn from Paul's situation is this. We may struggle with problems that we pray will disappear, and yet the Lord, who ultimately knows what is best for us, may, indeed, choose to say no. So how shall we respond?

Let's look at Paul's definition of grace. It is not merely pity or mercy or vague intentions of benevolence, but God's power, an enabling and sustaining energy arising out of His invincible determination to help us. What does Paul mean when he says it is in weakness that strength is made perfect? As hard as it is to believe, *human helplessness is its ideal context.*

This is where grace is seen in real glory, in the lives of those who feel hopelessly inadequate in the face of stress and duty and temptation. And isn't this exactly what the thorn did for Paul? It created a profound sense of insufficiency.

This brings up an interesting question. How often does God use hindrances to keep His people from depending on their flesh to do His will? Some very famous and effective evangelists have had to deal with this very issue. John Calvin had to preach while chronically ill. Charles Haddon Spurgeon was forced to preach in spite of constant pain and chronic depression. One of my pastor friends was married to a woman who suffered from mental illness, causing him untold grief and humiliation.

How often must these men have cried out to God, saying that if only these problems were removed, they could serve God ever so much more effectively? Yet for Paul the thorn was the very prerequisite necessary for effective ministry, driving him beyond himself to the Christ, through whom he could do all things.

Like Paul, we can process our feelings, coming to a place of rest with what God has allowed. Paul decided he was no longer going to waste time arguing for his own will, but instead would glory in the middle of the situation. With God's perspective on the situation, he was able to rejoice and be grateful for the struggle, knowing that in God's economy, that trial serves to change us in our inward man—to present us faultless before the presence of His glory with exceeding joy.

And like Paul, we might be exalted above measure without the existence of our trials. We need to recognize the danger of pride and rather endure the trial than fall into the sin of spiritual pride, which loves to steal the glory from God. The thorn served a purpose. It made self-confidence and self-reliance impossible. More than anything else, Paul takes great joy in the presence of affliction, "that the power of Christ may rest on me" (v. 9).

Let me conclude by saying this—if our goal to be of use to God, we must welcome the conditions necessary for our usefulness. The following poem sums it up beautifully. It is said to have been written by a soldier, while at war, but the author's name is unknown.

My Prayer

I asked for health that I might do greater things;
I was given infirmity that I might do better things.
I asked God for strength that I might achieve;
I was made weak that I might obey.
I asked for riches that I might be happy;
I was given poverty that I might be wise.
I asked for power and praise of men;
I was given weakness to sense my need of God.
I asked for all things that I might enjoy life;
I was given life that I might enjoy all things.
I got nothing I asked for but everything I hoped for;
In spite of myself, my prayers were answered–
I am among all men most richly blessed.

CHAPTER FIFTEEN

Jesus

saiah 53 (NIV) says this:

Who has believed our message and to whom has the arm of the Lord been revealed? He grew up before him like a tender shoot and like a root out of dry ground. He had no beauty or majesty to attract us to him, nothing in His appearance that we should desire him. He was despised and rejected by men, a man of sorrows, familiar with suffering. Like one from whom men hide their faces, He was despised and we esteemed him not. Surely he took up our infirmities and carried our sorrows, yet we considered him stricken by God, smitten by him, and afflicted. But he was pierced for our transgressions, He was crushed for our iniquities; the punishment that brought us peace was upon him, and by his wounds we are healed. All we, like sheep, have gone astray; each one of us has turned to his own way, and the Lord has laid on him the iniquity of us all. He was oppressed and afflicted, yet he did not open his mouth; he was led like a lamb to the slaughter, and as a sheep before her shearers is silent, so he did not open his mouth. By oppression and judgment, he was taken away. And who can speak of his descendents? For he was cut off from the land of the living; for the transgression of my people he was stricken. He was assigned a grave with the wicked, and with the rich in his death, though he had done no violence, nor was deceit in his mouth. Yet it was the Lord's will to crush him and cause him to suffer, and though the Lord makes his life a guilt offering, he will see his offspring and prolong his days, and the will of the Lord will prosper in his hand.

After the suffering of his soul, He will see the light of life and be satisfied, by his knowledge my righteous servant will justify man, and he will bear their iniquities.

Therefore will I give him a portion with the strong, because he poured out his life unto death, and was numbered with the transgressors. For he bore the sin of many and made intercession for the transgressors.

I come to the chapter on Jesus with fear and trembling. Not because God is going to judge me if I make a mistake, but because I stand in awe of Him and wonder how I, a novice, could do justice to writing about Him.

The movie, *The Passion of the Christ*, by Mel Gibson, has been released and depicts before our very eyes what can never be explained in mere words.

I have felt rejection all of my life. No on can tell or describe the pain of rejection; it has to be felt. When thinking about rejection, I recalled many experiences and tried to cover them all from every angle.

A woman told me that she and her son had a close bond throughout his childhood. But just before high school graduation he moved out, got an apartment, and told her he could have no communication with her whatsoever, all this without a sign or warning as to why. He shunned her completely for three devastating years. Then he decided to rebuild the relationship. She forgave him and they moved on. But a few years later, out of the blue, once again, he decided to cease all communication. This time the distancing lasted a little less than a year, but during that time the son got engaged. His mother was denied any contact with his fiancé or her family. He did not allow her to have an engagement celebration for them, and she was not invited to any of the pre-wedding festivities. She wasn't sure she would even be allowed to attend the wedding, but a couple of weeks before the date, she received an invitation. Although she was given the traditional place of honor at the ceremony, she was seated at the back of the room during the reception. Just before she left, she found a piece of paper describing the beach wedding that her son and his bride had two days before: their legal wedding. The bride's family and a few friends had attended the beach ceremony, but the groom hadn't even told his mother about it. This was a near fatal rejection to say the least.

When I went through divorce the hardest thing for me was rejection from friends. One niece-in-law told me right out, "Don't even come around our home. It hurts us too much to be reminded that you and my aunt are no longer together." Rejection hurts a lot. And my own foster son's wife made him tell me to "Get lost" after my divorce. She did not want me to be a part of their lives anymore. Divorce separates families on both sides. Rejection hurts so badly sometimes you just want to die. Jesus came unto His own and they were the very people who rejected Him.

One more illustration I'd like to give. This one brings tears to my eyes just writing it. A family had a daughter who graduated from high school. The daughter had problems during the teen years, as all kids do. But she graduated with honors and all the preparations were made to send her off to college. She did well the first semester and then she went back for her second semester. The family heard nothing from her, so after a long period of time they called the school and were informed that she was no longer enrolled there. They panicked. After what seemed like an eternity they finally heard from the daughter. She was pregnant and living with her boyfriend's parents.

After two more children, three in all, she told her parents she wanted nothing to do with them, to this date they have never seen their grand-daughter except for pictures—imagine the hurt and rejection. Rejection hurts right down to our innermost parts and beyond. To me this is the worst rejection that can be felt by any human being. But remember, this is nothing compared to the rejection Jesus suffered for all of us.

I can only imagine the rejection that Jesus felt when He came into this world and was rejected. But the passage in Isaiah says He didn't complain. "He was oppressed, *yet when* He was afflicted He was submissive *and* opened not His mouth; as a lamb that is led to the slaughter, and as a sheep that before her shearers is dumb, so He opened not His mouth" (Isaiah 53:7 Amplified Bible).

The cross was physical torture no man should have had to endure, and yet there was something much more terrible than that coming. His perfection took on the weight and stench of a foreign substance called sin. He who knew no sin, suddenly became sin for us.

"But these pains are a mere warm-up to His other and growing dread. He begins to feel a foreign sensation. Somewhere during this day an un-earthly foul odor began to waft. Not around his nose, but his heart. He *feels* dirty. Human wickedness starts to craw upon his spotless being—the living excrement from our souls. The apple of his father's eye turns brown with rot.

94

"His Father! Must he face his Father like this!

"From heaven the Father now rouses himself like a lion disturbed, shakes his mane, and roars against the shivering remnant of a man hanging on a cross. *Never* has the Son seen the Father look at him so, never felt even the least of his hot breath. But the roar shakes the unseen world and darkens the visible sky. The Son does not recognize these eyes.

"Son of man! Why have you behaved so? You have cheated, lusted, stolen, gossiped—murdered, envied, hated, lied. You have cursed, robbed, overspent, overeaten—fornicated, disobeyed, embezzled, and blasphemed. Oh, the duties you have shirked, the children you have abandoned! Who has ever so ignored the poor, so played the coward, so belittled my name? Have you *ever* held your razor tongue? What a self-righteous, pitiful drunk—*you,* who molest young boys, peddle killer drugs, travel in cliques, and mock your parents.. Who gave you the boldness to rig elections, ferment revolutions, torture animals and worship diamonds? Does the list never end! Splitting families, raping virgins, acting smugly, playing the pimp—buying politicians, practicing extortion, filming pornography, accepting bribes. You have burned down buildings, perfected terrorist tactics, founded false religions, traded in slaves—relishing each morsel and bragging about it all. I *hate, I loathe* these things in you! Disgust for everything about you consumes me! Can you not feel my wrath?'

"The Father watches as his heart's treasure, the mirror image of Himself, sinks drowning into raw, liquid sin. Jehovah's stored rage against humankind from every century explodes in a single direction.

"Father! Father! Why have you forsaken me?!"

"But heaven stops its ears. The Son stares up at the One who cannot, who will not, reach down or reply. Two eternal hearts tear—their intimate friendship shaken to the depths.

"The Trinity had planned it. The Son endured it. The Spirit enabled him. The Father rejected the son whom he loved. Jesus the God-man from Nazareth perished. The Father accepted his sacrifice for sin and was satisfied. The Rescue was accomplished.

"God set down his law.

"*This* is who asks us to trust him when he calls on us to suffer.[8]

My Vision

The point in time was over 20 years ago. I cannot tell you if this was a dream or a direct vision. I felt dry spiritually and wanted to get closer to Jesus Christ. I told my new wife that I was going on a fast from food until I heard from Him. I was starting my third day of the fast and I felt very tired and drained. I told Marian that I was going to lie down. I went to lie down and here's what I saw:

Jesus was being placed on the cross on the ground. The soldiers were ready to pound the nails into His hands. I walked over to where they were and simply asked Jesus, "Why?" He turned His head and looked straight into my eyes and with a smile on His wounded face and with compassion I could feel, He said, "I am doing this for you." I was standing on His left and as the soldier pounded the nail into His right hand I heard and felt the sound with my heart and I began to cry.

The vision was over. It must have taken a fraction of a second but it was real and when I get into a dry spell spiritually I remember our conversation. This vision has brought me through many hard times, even when I played the prodigal and left for the dredges of the world, I saw him being nailed to the cross for me, and it broke my heart and brought me back to my Father's waiting arms.

Jesus died, and the Father accepted His sacrifice for sin, and was satisfied. The Rescue was accomplished once and for all. Because Jesus suffered first and most of all, He asks us to trust Him when He calls us to suffering. Jesus died for our sins, but He rose from the dead and he is praying for us right now. Please give Him the best you have—your heart and life.

Part III

CHAPTER SIXTEEN

Childhood to Conversion Experience

F ood was cheap. Coffee sold for nineteen cents a pound, butter and bacon for twenty cents a pound. Sugar and flour cost twenty-five cents for five pounds, and a dollar would buy five gallons of gas.

"Black Tuesday," October 19, 1929, is the day everyone remembers because the stock market crashed, officially setting off what is known as "The Great Depression." As unemployment skyrocketed within the next four years, nearly a fourth of the workforce lost jobs, and many people became homeless. Times were tough, to say the least. Because President Herbert Hoover was at a loss to handle the crisis, Franklin D. Roosevelt was elected president and promised a "New Deal" for the now hopeful American people. Congress created the Works Progress Administration (WPA), which offered work relief for a vast number of people.

My parents, Mary Grace and Edward Lindenberger, worked through those difficult years, proud that they never took one cent of charity along the way, in spite of the fact that they had seven children.

With Dad's gardening talents and Mother's canning skills, they were able to feed our family in the years before my birth.

They could almost see the end of the tunnel financially, when they received a new and stunning blow. Another child was on the way, to make a total of eight.

How does a family endure the Great Depression and now face a dilemma of such magnitude? My father, in his infinite wisdom, came up with a solution.

Mother would simply have to go to work after the baby came.

On February 3, 1935, the baby boy was born. Five older sisters greeted him with great excitement.

It looked like the baby would go nameless until the day the insurance man came to add his name to the family policy. When he asked his mother for baby's name, she had no answer, so the man said, "I'll just put down Robert Ivan." So little Robert grew into his name, and soon his mother left his sisters in charge, while she went to work. When my youngest sister, Mary, was old enough to attend school, I stayed in the care of my aunt, who lived next door. One of her two sons volunteered to watch me, and though I was only five, I already knew my older cousin was up to no good. He asked me to watch and do things that no five year old should see or do.

A coal oil stove and a space heater heated our home, and my toy box was visible through the floor vent that opened to the bathroom upstairs.

One day I heard my mother scream and cry, so I looked through the vent and saw her sitting atop my toy box, with her hands covering her face. Running down the stairs I found a crowd in the living room and felt confused, concerned about my mom. I had never seen her so upset. Later I learned that terror had fueled her fretful outburst, as she worried about my two older brothers, who were of draft age on that fateful winter day—the day Japan attacked Pearl Harbor.

Because I was small for my age and a bit slower than my peers, I had trouble keeping up, and struggled with the ridicule of classmates and even teachers on occasion, so it's no wonder I hated school.

At home, I was happy and thrived, except that I was often compared to my two older brothers, and always came up wanting. After deciding I could never live up to their example, I forged an identity of my own. I developed a reputation for being stubborn and difficult, but at least this identity was all mine.

Early childhood hearing loss, the result of repeated painful ear infections, wasn't discovered until after I had been labeled retarded by many of the adults in my world.

In fact, my hearing loss was first discovered and named by a sharp and observant coach, who finally realized the cause of my struggle. Seeing my potential for football, he worked with me, teaching me how to watch the ball, and ultimately turned me into a competent and confident member of the team. At least until a new coach came and once again labeled me retarded.

Hurt and humiliated, I acted out in anger, causing my own problems, and basically shooting myself in the foot, until a new kid moved into the area. We became fast friends, and under his influence I settled down and began, once again, to feel pride in being me.

After high school, I spent a short time working, before I joined the Navy, choosing that branch of service simply because my idol, my brother-in-law, had been a Navy man. It was time for me to make my mark on the world, proving to my detractors that I was not a failure. After struggling through boot camp, I was assigned to Class A school, where I trained as a machinist's mate. It was there that I was first introduced to the Bible and prayer. And though I would not come to know Christ for some time, that time left a deep impression on my heart. After graduation, they assigned me to a refrigeration ship, which would supply the U.S. fleet with food while at sea.

Being away from home for the first time in my life was a heady experience. I couldn't help wanting to prove myself in front of my peers, so I tried it all, and it wasn't long before I gained the dubious distinction as the ship's token drunken sailor. Aboard ship, I worked hard, living for the moment I would be free to go ashore and have fun. Then something happened to change that.

Our ship, the U.S.S. Alstede, had just come out of dry-dock after repairs at Staten Island Harbor, New York, and was sent on what is called a shakedown cruise. A shakedown, like a dry run, was designed to expose problems that would need further repair before the ship actually headed out to sea.

On this shakedown, we picked up a chaplain in Gitmo, Cuba who was returning to the states. While on board, he held services in the mess hall each night. A fellow sailor repeatedly invited me to go, but I refused, not the least bit interested in God's opinion of my life. I knew I wasn't living right, so why would I ask for trouble?

In spite of my refusal, my shipmate continued to invite me, until one night I went, simply to get him off my back.

Though I don't recall a single word the chaplain said that night, the Holy Spirit's voice made a deep and lasting impression, breaking my heart over my sin. When, after the service, the chaplain confronted me about being a Christian. He asked, "Are you a Christian? I told him I was a member of the Brethren Church.

He asked again, "Are you a Christian?"

I hung my head.

Opening his Bible, he read what I later learned was John 3:15, which says, "As Moses lifted up the serpent in the wilderness, so the Son of man shall be lifted up." When he asked me if I understood that verse, I had to admit I did not.

He explained, "The Children of Egypt had been slaves in Egypt until God told Moses to lead them out of slavery through the Red Sea. And not long after, while in the desert, many people were dying from the bite of deadly snakes. God told Moses to make a snake of gold, attach it to a pole, and hold it high in the air. Anyone bitten by the snakes could look up at the snake on the pole and be healed.

Then he asked me something strange. He wanted to know—if I had been a snakebite victim at the time, would I have looked up at the snake to be healed. I said yes, and he went on to explain that many died because of their stubborn refusal to follow the simple directive to look.

He added that I could look up to Jesus, who had died and been lifted up, and he would heal me from my sins.

Though I didn't receive Jesus Christ as my Savior that night, the seeds of conviction were already being sown in my heart.

When we returned stateside, the same seaman who invited me to the chaplain's service asked me to attend a Youth for Christ meeting with him at the Norfolk YMCA. A Billy Graham film shown there focused on my need to receive Christ, and, unable to withstand the wooing of the Spirit, I became a child of God.

Here is the message Billy brought that night. It was nearly fifty years ago, but I will never forget its haunting words:

In the world in which we live, we give most attention to satisfying the appetites of the body and practically none to the soul. Consequently, we are one-sided. We become fat physically and materially, while spiritually we are lean, weak and anemic.

The soul actually demands as much attention as the body. It demands fellowship, and common communion with God. It demands worship, quietness, and meditation. Unless the soul is fed and exercised daily, it becomes weak and shriveled.

It remains discontented, confused and restless. Many people turn to alcohol to tame the craving and longings of the soul. Some turn to sex experiences. Others attempt to quiet the longings of their souls in other ways.

But nothing but God ever completely satisfies, because the soul was made for God, and without God, it is restless and in secret torment."

—Billy Graham, Hour of Power Film, 1955

This ship's drunk, with a mouth like a cesspool, returned to the ship a changed man and began witnessing to anyone who would listen. Some just smiled and said it wouldn't last. Others did more than smile; they laughed out loud. What had happened to me? Why was there such a drastic change?

I was redeemed by the blood of Christ. I was justified in God's sight, which means He now looked at me just-as-if-I'd-never-sinned. I was sanctified, set apart for His use, and made holy as He is holy.

I had been given eternal life, and could now be sure that my eternal future was secured in heaven. That is salvation.

CHAPTER SEVENTEEN

The Simple Plan of Salvation

God made man for fellowship with Himself
Adam, the first man, was disobedient and chose to sin.
He placed sin on us.
We are guilty.
Because of our guilt, we deserve death.
Christ died in our place.
We admit we are guilty.
We believe Christ was punished in our place.
We are declared "not guilty."

Sin brought about the need for man's salvation. Sin is like a genetic disease that, once introduced into the human race, affected everyone thereafter. Sin separates us from a Holy God, but in the Bible we see the story of God's remedy for the problem of sin in our individual lives and the whole of creation. It describes a perfect creation in the Garden of Eden and a terrible fall from grace, due to Adam and Eve's disobedience to the divine command of a sovereign God. In salvation we find a victorious remedy called redemption, found in the person of the obedient Son, Jesus Christ. There is also a vibrant Christ-like holiness for the child of God who is obedient. And finally, there is a glorious hope that when Christ comes again, we shall be like Him and enjoy Him forever.

Therefore, just as sin entered into the world through one man, and death through sin, and in this way death came to all men, because all sinned (Romans 5:12 KJV).

The "one man" spoken of here is Adam. His sin poisoned the human race. Every man, woman and child born since Adam has been born a sinner. Sin goes deeper than merely an association with some distant relative (original sin). In fact, it has contaminated our very nature. Every man since Adam was born with the inclination to sin as well as a bias away from good.

If you don't believe me, ask any preschool worker or kindergarten teacher. Children never need a lesson in being bad. It comes naturally. Granted, some are worse than others. But each child, in his or her own way, eventually demonstrates a defiant egocentrism that will challenge all comers.

God created Adam in His own likeness, perfect and without sin. But when Adam disobeyed God, sin entered the world, shattering that original intimate relationship between God and man, and changing the nature of man for all time. Because of that sin, all men since Adam have been born in sin, separated from God. Isaiah 59:2 says, *Your iniquities have made a separation between you and your God, and your sins have hidden His face from you...*

After Adam made the choice to disobey, the characteristics that reflected God's personality were changed, corrupted in all mankind, leaving only a dim memory of what might have been. And from that point on, man's world was also corrupted by the entrance of sin. This is what scripture calls the "fall of man." So it is that all men remain under the power of sin until delivered by the awesome power of God.

In his book, *The Saving Life of Christ*, Major W. Ian Thomas says this:

> At the fall of man, when Adam sinned, God withdrew His Holy Spirit from the human spirit, and although man retained his animal body and possessed still a functioning soul of mind, emotion and will, he was empty of God. Spiritually bankrupt, man was destitute of that spiritual life which could be his only by virtue of God's presence, through His Holy Spirit, within the human spirit. God had left him!
> This was the consequence of sin—the absence of all spiritual life means spiritual death. This is the wages of sin; not the ultimate consequence of

sin one day, but that which has been the consequence of sin ever since man fell and that which is now the condition of sin to all who have not as yet been saved from this condition, for in this condition of spiritual death that we are all born, easy prey to the ravages of a sin principle that came into the human heart in the day that God went out.[9]

In 1 John 3:4, it says, *Everyone who sins breaks the law; in fact, sin is lawlessness.*(NIV) The combination of our inherent sinfulness and our ensuing acts of sin alienates us from a sovereign God. The Bible goes so far as to say we are condemned:

Again the gift is not like the result of the one man's sin; the judgment followed one sin and brought condemnation (Romans 5:16 NIV).

The word condemn is a legal term meaning "to declare guilty." We are each guilty of sin—both from our relationship with Adam, otherwise referred to as original sin, and those resulting from personal disobedience.

Just as sin separated Adam and Eve from God in the beginning, sin continues to separate mankind from God, both now and for eternity, exclusive of man's change of heart in response to God's sacrificial gift of Jesus.

For the wages of sin is death.

(Romans 6:23 KJV)

For all have sinned and fall short of the glory of God.

(Romans 3:23 KJV)

These familiar scripture passages clear up many questions regarding the consequences of sin. Note that when the Bible speaks of death, it does not refer to annihilation of the soul. Once conceived, every soul will survive for eternity, in either heaven or hell. In this case, the word death refers to eternal separation of the soul from the presence of a loving God. Because God is holy and pure in nature, He cannot tolerate the presence of sin. And because of our sin nature, He cannot fellowship with those of us who are still in a sinful state of being. Those who want intimate fellowship with their Creator must be declared guiltless, restored to right relationship with God, having accepted God's sacrificial gift of salvation.

This situation is not due to an arbitrary set of rules God dictated simply to make life difficult for us, but rather we might say that the rules were already in place when our sovereign God hung the stars. The advent of sin suddenly shed light on the awful truth that God and man no longer had anything in common with each other. With such a gaping chasm between us, how can a holy God communicate with mortal man?

This lesson was made clear one day while we were picnicking. We ate on a blanket on the ground and, as sometimes happens, left crumbs in our wake. Shortly an army of ants appeared as if by magic and began to haul them off.

We watched the progress as a single ant returned repeatedly, picked up a crumb and carried it to his hole in the ground.

Wanting to help, we decided to offer him an entire hotdog roll, so we placed it in his path, where he couldn't miss seeing it. We even spoke to him, offering our help. Instead of accepting our gift, he walked around it and over it, but it was no use. We could not communicate. We were too big and he was too small. The only way to help the ant was to become an ant and pick up a crumb and begin to communicate with him on his level.

In the same way, Jesus obeyed the Father and came to earth to show us what God was like and to communicate with us on our level. Had He not used this approach, we would have scampered away, unable to understand God, simply because of our inability to understand. He came as an infant in a manger, because that was something with which we could easily identify. Had he not been obedient to come in human form, we could never have understood God.

CHAPTER EIGHTEEN

Redemption

Because of sin, mankind had a need. Someone needed to come and bridge that huge, gaping chasm between God and man, restoring the intimate fellowship for which God had created him.

The dictionary defines the word "redeem" this way. "To buy back or a) set free by paying a ransom; b) to deliver from sin and its penalties, as by sacrifice made for the sinner. And to fulfill a promise or pledge."

Let's review the words used to define "redeem." "Buy back; repay; ransom; reclaim; retrieve; regain; recover; discharge; restore; reinstate; recapture; and repossess." These words explain exactly what Jesus Christ did for us by willingly going to the cross.

Because Jesus went to the cross, it is now possible for the Holy Spirit to communicate with the hearts of men and awaken him to his need for a savior.

I had no idea that the way I was living was an offense to God, that is, until the Holy Spirit revealed my need. He shined a light on my sins, put them in perspective for me, and then showed me the solution to the problem. My responsibility, at that point, was to respond to the tender wooing of the Spirit and confess my sins, agreeing with God's opinion on the subject, and then turn around and go the way of righteousness.

CHAPTER NINETEEN

Justification

Justification is an amazing concept—the complete forgiveness of sin, to where God not only forgives what I've done in the past, but forgets it ever happened in the first place. He then looks at me with new eyes, the eyes of the Spirit, seeing me perfect, just as if I'd never sinned.

Once a young man stood in court, waiting to appear before the judge for a felony he had committed. He was found guilty of a serious offense, for which the fine was $500. The judge banged his gavel to adjourn the court, then stood and removed his judge's robe. While everyone watched, he approached the bailiff and proceeded to pay the fine himself. The guilty man was free to go, his fine paid in full.

In fact, the judge was the young man's father. In the eyes of the law, the penalty for wrongdoing was paid in full. And just like the law changed the way it viewed the young man after his fine was paid, justification is a change in God's attitude toward us after Jesus' blood covers our sin.

CHAPTER TWENTY

Regeneration

The term 'regeneration' describes an actual change that takes place in us when we accept the terms of salvation, a contract wherein the fine is paid in full, by the blood of Jesus. The Bible calls this event being "born-again." It isn't just a change of mind, like turning over a new leaf, but is a complete transformation, the death of the old spirit and the birth of something brand new. And it can only happen when we believe what God has said and accept His gift of salvation by faith.

I like the story of the man who strung a wire over Niagara Falls. He put a wheelbarrow on the wire and walked across, pushing it in front of him. When he reached the other side, a huge crowd had gathered to applaud and welcome him. He asked if they believed he could once again cross safely to the other side. They enthusiastically agreed that he could, but when he asked for a volunteer to sit in the wheelbarrow, there were no volunteers. No one trusted him enough to go with him. The person who honestly desires a relationship with God, and believes in faith, will receive this same regeneration. *Whoever believeth that Jesus is the Christ is born of God* (1 John 5:1 KJV).

CHAPTER TWENTY ONE

Adoption

At the point where we accept the gift of salvation, we also become a part of a new family.

...those who are led by the Spirit of God are sons of God...you received the Spirit of sonship. The Spirit himself testifies with our spirit that we are God's children. Now if we are children, then we are heirs—heirs of God and co-heirs with Christ, if indeed we share in his sufferings in order that we may also share in his glory (Romans 8:14-17 NIV).

Adoption involves not only being part of the family but also taking the family name and becoming an heir, with a future guarantee of the inheritance. Once born again, we take His name, and now go by the name Christian. Being called by His name also demands we assume the responsibility of that status.

Because this Father never dies, He has already given us our inheritance.

CHAPTER TWENTY TWO

Conversion

In my younger days, I bought a conversion van. It had no windows, and had been designed for hauling. The man who converted it stripped out everything inside and added carpet, sleeping quarters, a stove, sink and refrigerator.

Just like that van was converted from the inside out, so man is changed from the inside out when God takes control. I had an uncontrollable temper before I met Jesus Christ as my Lord and Savior. I remember well how I could be provoked to a fight with just a wrong look or a misconstrued word. After I received Christ I was amazed at the change in my life. I stopped the drinking and tried to get along with everyone.

One of my best buddies on the ship teased me unmercifully after my conversion and actually yelled at me one day when I came into the engine room, "Convert me, brother." I looked at him with a serious face and asked him what that word meant. He didn't know and I was a brand new Christian, so neither did I. So together we went to the library and looked the word conversion up. Here is what we discovered:

1   a converting or being converted; specif.,
  a) a change from lack of faith to a religious belief; adoption of a religion b) a change from one belief, religion, doctrine, opinion, etc. to another

My shipmate read this and looked at me and said, "So that's what happened to you?"

Conversion is: "A basic change in belief, especially, espousal of a religion and it has many ways to say it. Spiritual change, regeneration, rebirth, accepting the true faith, turning to the church, turning to God, turning to Christ, being born again, being baptized, seeing the light, change of heart, change in character, and new birth." You could add some of your own phrases but it all adds up to drastic change in a person's life.

CHAPTER TWENTY THREE

Sanctification/Holiness

If you recall, I mentioned being the ship's drunk before my conversion. Does that mean that I never sinned again?

In truth, I was changed in the twinkling of an eye, changed so that I no longer had a bent toward sin and things God hated, but the old sin nature, the ability to sin, was and is still present.

But from God's point of view, salvation is the point where we are no longer who we once were. We take on a new name, a new personality, and scripture says we are made holy through the sacrifice of Christ. His blood, in fact, transforms the vilest sinner into someone holy and perfect before God. *But of Him are ye in Christ Jesus, who of God is made for us wisdom, and righteousness, and sanctification, and redemption–But you are washed, but you are sanctified, but you are justified in the name of the Lord Jesus, and by the Spirit of our God* (1 Corinthians 1:30; 6:11 KJV). This means he has been separated from his past life and is now dedicated to God.

The Bible is clear in its teaching that Christians should continue living a life that is separated from sin and dedicated to God, because this is His will for them. *Since we have these promises, dear friends, let us purify ourselves from everything that contaminates body and spirit, perfecting holiness out of reverence for God* (2 Corinthians 7:1 NIV).

It is God's will that you should be sanctified...that each of you should learn to control his own body in a way that is holy and honorable... (1 Thessalonians 4:3 NIV).

These verses describe what is called the progressive aspect of sanctification. The Bible also speaks of it as growing in grace. *Like newborn babies, crave pure spiritual milk, so that by it you may grow up in your salvation.* (1 Peter 2:2 NIV). And in 1 Corinthians 3, it also discusses the believer's gradual spiritual transformation.

Progressive sanctification is the process whereby believers become more like Jesus Christ. It is our responsibility to make every effort to live a holy life, because the Bible says, *without holiness no one will see the Lord* (Hebrews 12:14 NIV).

We must see holiness as a process that has a starting point at salvation, where we are gloriously saved and once more restored to right relationship with God. At that point, we are set apart for fellowship with Him. From that point on, we are in the process of being conformed to His likeness.

The little song, *He's Still Working On Me,* by Joel Hemphill says it best:

There really aught to be a sign upon the heart,
Don't judge her yet, there's an unfinished part.
But I'll be perfect just according to His plan
Fashioned by the Master's loving hands.

In the mirror of His word reflections that I see
Make me wonder why He never gave up on me.
He loves me as I am and helps me when I pray
Remember He's the potter, I'm the clay.

He's still working on me to make me what I ought to be.
It took Him just a week to make the moon and stars,
The Sun and the earth and Jupiter and Mars.
How loving and patient He must be, He's still working on me.

Sanctification takes place at the moment of salvation and then must continue as the believer submits to the control of the Holy Spirit.

The tragedy of the church today is that it fails to teach the whole truth and tends to stop with the past tense salvation experience, encouraging no one to keep growing in stature with God and man.

If we believe this half-truth, we are in danger of thinking we've got it made, since we've been saved, and can now choose to live as we please, failing to see that our old man is no better now that he was before, unless he is submitting continuously to the power of the Holy Spirit.

Sad to say, but many churches are breeding grounds for sin, because of this type of teaching. These misguided saints are resting on the finished work of Jesus Christ while living like the devil, which means they are out from under authority and are in danger of throwing away their salvation. Let me share a perfect example from my days in the service.

After I accepted Christ and became a new person, with new desires, an old drinking buddy approached me and asked if I wanted to go ashore and drink with him.

I told him I was a Christian and didn't care to drink anymore. He said, "No sweat. I'm a Christian, too."

I asked him to explain, and he told me a sad but commonly heard story.

"In Norfolk, I met a pretty girl and asked her to go to the movies with me. She said, 'I can't go out with you. You're not a Christian. You're not saved.'

"So I asked her, 'What must I do to be saved?' She said, 'Believe on the Lord Jesus Christ, and you will be saved', and I said, 'I believe.'

"She said, 'Good. You're saved. Now we can go to the movies.'"

This is only one example of what I call 'easy believe-ism'. I have to ask myself, Where is the godly sorrow for sin? Where is the changed heart? Did he really believe Jesus had died for him? Was he really made holy and set apart to God when he simply said he believed? When I asked him these questions, he simply shook his head and said he had no idea what I was talking about.

The cross is only the beginning for a new believer. The cross is the point in time when we are instantly made alive to spiritual things, but we must continue on, being made holy on an ongoing basis, which is why we must continually renew our old mind, transforming its logic to conform with the truth of scripture.

CHAPTER TWENTY FOUR

The Bible is Truth

It is a good thing to pursue knowledge. But knowledge without truth will benefit little, because it causes man to be puffed up with pride. This kind of knowledge will do nothing to reveal to him the truth of God.

What is truth?

Solomon said, "The fear of the Lord is the beginning of knowledge" (Proverbs 1:7 KJV). We must understand the relationship between God and the truth as God sees it.

Without the Holy Spirit and the instruction of God's Word, man will never really "get it." In fact, 2 Timothy 3:7 describes it this way: "learning and never able to come to knowledge of the truth."

When we acknowledge and obey His truth, however, we will be set free from spiritual error and our own form of truth. Only diligent study of God's Word will give us the whole truth of God.

To summarize, the blood of Jesus has already made us holy, but holiness must not stop there. As long as we are on earth, we must each work out our own salvation, submitting to the will of God. We will never be perfect as long as we have our old bodies and our old minds, which are limited, but when we are submitted to the Holy Spirit, He will continue the work of changing us into the likeness of Christ.

The written Word of God cannot fail to change us as we read it, study it, and apply it to our lives. Within its pages is the truth, which is the power of God. The Word is a living entity, and when we read it, it transforms our minds, our emotions and our wills. In so doing, it also changes our thinking and our conduct. The Word of God forms the nature of God within us, building God's character into our character. The more we drench ourselves in God's Word, the more we are transformed into His likeness, and the more power we have over our old man and his old belief system. We must agree that a life without the constant input of the scriptures is a life with no power at all. 1 Thessalonians 2:13 (NIV) says ...*the word of God, which is at work in you who believe.* It is the Word of God in us, which makes us holy. Much Word, then, equals much power. No Word equals no power.

I can move furniture to the second floor of my home, but not without help, and the same is true in our spiritual life. Jesus knew we could not live a victorious life here on earth without Him or His Word.

The enemy of our souls, Satan, is alive and well on the planet Earth and is walking back and forth seeking all those he can trap and devour, leading them away from God.

Jesus said, *If you love me, you will obey what I command. And I will ask the Father, and He will give you another Counselor to be with you forever—the Spirit of truth. The world cannot accept him, because it neither sees nor knows him. But you know him, for he lives with you and will be in you. I will not leave you orphans; I will come to you. Before long, the world will not see me anymore, but you will see me. Because I live, you also will live* (John 14:15-19 NIV).

CHAPTER TWENTY FIVE

The Holy Spirit

A baby is born without knowledge of a Creator God. He or she has a sinful nature. In time, the Holy Spirit opens the eyes of the spirit to see the need for help, in the person of Jesus Christ.

Major W. Ian Thomas states it this way in his book *The Saving Life of Christ:*

> God in righteousness has no option but to find you guilty as a sinner—by nature dead in trespasses and sins—to pass upon you the sentence of death, the forfeiture of His Holy Spirit, and alienation from the life of God. But more than nineteen hundred years ago, God in Christ stepped out of eternity into time, and extended to you today the nail-pierced hands of One who suffered, "the just for the unjust," to bring you back to God (1 Peter 3:18a). He bore "our sins in his own body on a tree" (1 Peter 2:24a)...
>
> Your response to Jesus Christ will determine your condition in the sight of God—redeemed or condemned!
>
> *This, however, is but the beginning of the story, "for if, when we were enemies, we were reconciled {now an accomplished fact} we shall be saved {as a continuing process}...by his life"* (Romans 5:10). The glorious fact of the matter is this: no sooner has God reconciled to Himself the man who has responded to His call, than He reimparts to him as a forgiven sinner, the *presence of the Holy Spirit,* (emphasis mine) and this restoration to him of the Holy Spirit constitutes what the Bible calls regeneration, or new birth.

Titus 3:5-6 says, Not by works of righteousness which we have done, but according to his mercy he saved us, by the washing of regeneration, and the renewing of the Holy Ghost; which he shed on us abundantly through Jesus Christ our Savior.[10]

John 16:8 says, "*When he comes, he will convict the world in regard to sin, and righteousness, and judgment; concerning sin, because men do not believe in me; and concerning righteousness, because I am going to the Father, where you can see me no longer; and in regard to judgment, because the prince of this world now stands condemned*" (NIV).

The work of the Holy Spirit is to convict, cleanse, guide, and give power to witness. The Holy Spirit does convict sinners; and when they repent, He will cleanse their hearts. He cannot, however, give power to the unrepentant, for they do not belong to Him.

Jesus was talking to the disciples in John 14:6, 7 when He said; "*I am the way, the truth and the life. No one comes to the Father, except through me. If you really knew me, you would know my father as well. From now on you do know Him and have seen him*" (NIV).

Jesus said that He was the light of the world. (John 3:19-21) "*This is the verdict: Light has come into the world, but men love darkness instead of the light, because their deeds were evil. Everyone who does evil hates the light, and will not come into the light for fear that his deeds will be exposed. But whoever lives by the truth comes into the light, so that they may be seen plainly that what he has done has been done through God*" (NIV).

Let's examine the concept of light and darkness. Have you ever asked yourself when the lights are on—where the darkness has gone? We can postulate and reason, but we always come short of understanding, because there really is no answer.

So what really happens when we turn on the lights? We can finally see.

CHAPTER TWENTY SIX

What Is Light?

At a certain college, a professor had a reputation for being tough on Christians. At the first class of each semester, he would ask Christians to identify themselves and then proceed to mock their faith.

One day he pointed to a student and asked the question, "Did God make everything, young man?"

He replied enthusiastically, "Yes, sir. He did!"

The professor retorted, "Then if God made everything, He also made evil."

The student had no answer, and the professor grinned gleefully, having once again proven the Christian faith to be a myth.

Just then, another student raised his hand. "May I ask you something, sir?"

With the professor's assent, the student went on, "Sir, is there such a thing as cold?"

Looking greatly annoyed, the professor retorted, "Of course there is. What kind of a question is that? Haven't you ever been cold?"

The young man replied, "Actually, sir, cold doesn't exist. What we consider to be cold is really the absence of heat. Absolute zero is when there is absolutely no heat, but cold does not really exist. We have only created that term to describe how we feel when heat is not there."

The young man continued, "Sir, is there such a thing as dark?"

The professor responded, "Of course there is."

Once again, the student replied, "Actually, sir, darkness does not exist. Darkness is only the absence of light. Darkness is only a term man developed to describe what happens when there is no light present."

Finally the young man asked, "Sir, is there such a thing as evil?"

The professor replied, "Of course. We have rapes and murders and violence everywhere in the world. Those things are evil."

The student patiently replied, "Actually, sir—evil does not exist." Evil is simply the absence of God. Evil is a term man developed to describe the absence of God. God did not create evil. It isn't like truth or love, which exist as virtues like heat or light. Evil is simply the state where God is not present, like cold without heat or darkness without light."

As you can imagine, the professor had nothing to say...

I try to be a tidy person, but it seems that at the most inopportune time, I find myself dropping food on my white shirt.

This happened not long ago at a wedding reception. The lights were lowered for ambience, and at that point, all was well. We had just finished our meal, when the dessert was served. Shortly afterward, the lights were turned up, and I found myself covered with dessert down the front of my shirt. Would it have helped if I had requested the lights remain dimmed? No. The stain would still be on my shirt. The light illuminates what is already there.

Applying this in a spiritual sense, I can agree that before salvation came along, I was a sinner by nature. Because Adam and Eve sinned, I was also a sinner. While I had no relationship with a Holy God, the Holy Spirit shed light on my hopelessly lost spiritual condition, letting me see my need for Jesus. At that point, I could either choose to accept Jesus' sacrifice for sin, which would permanently remove the stain of sin, or I could choose to ask that the lights be turned off, so I wouldn't have to see the stain anymore. Only one of these methods deals with things the way they really are. The other simply uses a form of denial, pretending the problem away.

Jesus said, "I am the light of the world. Whoever follows me will never walk in darkness, but will have the light of life (John 8:12 NIV).

In his book, *The Holy Spirit*, evangelist Billy Graham quotes J. Gresham Machen as saying,

> "There must be a mysterious work of the Spirit of God in the new birth. Without that all or our arguments are quite useless... What the Holy Spirit does in the new birth is not to make a man a Christian regardless of the

evidence, but on the contrary to clear away the mists from our eyes and enable him to attend to the evidence."

This then is the meaning of the phrase used by Jesus when He said, "No man can come to me, except the Father which hath sent me draw him..."

(John 6:44 KJV)

To say we are living in the Spirit means living every moment as if you were actually standing in the presence of Jesus Christ. The very heart of the Spirit-filled life entails having your every thought yielded to Christ. God isn't necessarily interested in future commitments, but the here and now.

What if a man's wife came to him and said, "Honey, do you love me?"

If he's smart, he wouldn't reply, "Why don't you ask me a week from Sunday?"

She's not interested in how he will feel in the future. She wants to know how he feels right now. God is the same way. He's wholly interested in what we believe right now, and the truth is that being in the Holy Spirit, we are being filled now, in this very instant, as well as on into the future, with no gaps in between.

The Apostle Paul described a wonderful by-product of being Spirit-filled. "*And we, who with unveiled faces all reflect the Lord's glory, are being transformed into his likeness with ever-increasing glory, which comes from the father, who is the Spirit*" (2 Corinthians 3:18 NIV).

As you gaze at the glory of the Lord, focusing solely on Christ, you will be changed into His image by the Holy Spirit.

Christ-consciousness leads to Christ likeness. As you are continuously filled with the Holy Spirit, you become increasingly more like Christ.

When you function in your flesh, apart from the Holy Spirit, there will be no progress or maturity in your Christian life, leaving your spiritual growth stunted, only a pitiful reminder of what might have been.

The key to living the Christian life is to grow in Christ likeness as you are continually renewed in your mind by the Word of God and by the power of the Holy Spirit, ultimately resulting in power and victory.

What exactly does scripture mean when it talks about being filled with the Spirit?

Filling a glass to the top causes it to eventually overflow. The scripture also talks about how the disciple's nets were filled to overflowing with fish to where they were afraid the nets would tear.

When we are filled with God's Spirit, the vessel of our life is filled with God's presence until it overflows, pouring out of us.

Another meaning for the word 'fill' is to 'diffuse throughout'. The perfume of the woman who anointed Jesus filled the entire house, saturating every corner of the space. When the Holy Spirit fills us, His presence permeates every nook and cranny of our being, penetrating and scrutinizing every area of our lives. When we speak of filling our minds with God's Word, we mean that scripture must take possession of our minds until it controls us. In this sense, the word "fill" means "to dominate or take authority." God intended that the Holy Spirit flow out of us, touching everyone we meet.

Right before He ascended to heaven after His resurrection, Jesus said to His disciples, *when the Holy Spirit comes on you... you will be my witnesses in Jerusalem, and in all Judea and Samaria, and to the ends of the earth.*

Jesus had already commissioned the disciples to go and saturate the world with the truth of the gospel, and yet now He told them they couldn't do it alone, but would need more power to accomplish such an overwhelming task. In fact, they would need to be empowered by the Holy Spirit of God in order to be effective. Incredibly, though they had watched Jesus preach, as well as heal the sick and raise the dead, that knowledge would not be enough without the power of the Spirit.

Tragically, many Christians do not even know who the Holy Spirit is. Or if they do, they do not know how to appropriate His power, and that lack of understanding renders them powerless to obtain the abundant and fruitful life Christ intended.

Consider the amazing contrast between Christ's church today and the church of the first century. In his introduction to the *Letters to the Young Churches*, J. B. Phillips writes:

> The great difference between present-day Christianity and that of which we read in these letters, the New Testament epistles, is that to us, it is primarily a performance; to them it was a real experience. We are apt to reduce the Christian religion to a code or, at best, a rule of heart and life. To these men, it is quite plainly the invasion of their lives by a new quality of life together. They do not hesitate to describe this as Christ living in them.

What is the purpose of being filled with God's Spirit?

God fills you, not simply *to do*, but *to be*.

What you are is infinitely more important to God than anything you will ever do in His name. The Holy Spirit's presence and power in your life enables you to become like Christ and to live a holy life.

Sometimes it seems impossible to be holy in thought, word and deed, but when God fills you with His Spirit, you enter a process that conforms you to His image and likeness.

God fills you *to know*. He provides the means for you to know Him in a deeper way, one that is not just assent to what you have heard, but one where you can say, "I've been there myself, so I know."

God fills you *to serve*. God has a special plan for each of us that only finds fulfillment when we submit to the power of His Spirit. In the power of the Spirit, you will be able to do things as a part of, and for the body of Christ, that you cannot do apart from that Spirit. So does this mean the Spirit leaves when we fall into sin and walk away from God?

No, a thousand times no.

At the moment of salvation, the Holy Spirit comes to us. This is the beginning of a lifelong and ongoing relationship with God and His Spirit.

A good illustration of this point is a cistern, a system of collecting water that must be refreshed and renewed over time with rain. If rain is in short supply, a huge truckload of water has to refill the cistern.

And just like the cistern, the supply of the living water of God is also used up and needs to be constantly replenished. This happens when we open ourselves afresh to the Holy Spirit, asking Him to pour into us. The command in Ephesians 5:8 is this: Keep on keeping on being filled with the Spirit (my paraphrase).

In summary, the Spirit-filled life is the secret of the abundant life, a continuous process of receiving and giving, of being filled and sharing with others in the service of the Lord Jesus Christ.

CHAPTER TWENTY SEVEN

Forgiveness

There are four essential steps involved in forgiveness:

1. Hurt
2. Hate
3. Healing
4. Happiness (restoration)

Remember the story I shared about the high school coach who labeled me as retarded?

Once the label had been applied, I could do nothing right, in this man's eyes.

Because of my hearing impairment, I wasn't able to hear the snap of the football, so I never made my offensive blocks. This only confirmed the coach's negative belief system.

During a scrimmage right before our first game, I was anxious to prove myself, and ended up trying too hard. Eagerly blocking the center who was about to snap the ball, I accidentally broke his nose.

Now furious, the center came after me in the locker room, ready to beat me senseless. When he swung at me, I lowered my head, and he unknowingly broke three fingers on his right hand in his effort to injure me.

When the game started, he was hurting too much to stay in the game, so the coach told me to help him to the bench. I ran out to where he was, eager to help, picked him up like a little boy, and ran to the sidelines, where I settled him on the bench. The coach turned and yelled at me, cursed, and in anger told me to get out of his sight and go get dressed. He called me a 'retard' in front of the entire stadium. His words humiliated me, yet I had no idea what I had done wrong.

This same coach was also our health and physical education teacher, and because he believed I was retarded, he assigned me to the class with the slower students. In one class, he was teaching us boxing and had me put on the gloves and box with several other students. Because of my size and ability, I was able to overcome each of them.

In anger, the coach sent our star quarterback, an agile, imposing guy, in to box with me. When I once again landed the right punches, the coach lost control of his anger, and donned the gloves himself, punching and pounding me until I could no longer see. If the class had not stopped him, he would have killed me in his fury. Not surprisingly, I was *hurt*, both physically and emotionally, at his hand. As a result, I also learned the meaning of the word *hate*. I carried this baggage with me through the rest of high school and into the Navy.

After accepting Jesus as Savior, I still had a boatload of hate for this man. In fact, I liked nothing more than reviewing in my mind the list of ways I could get even, repaying injury for injury.

Over time, the Holy Spirit began convicting me of my vengeful attitude, reminding me that Jesus had forgiven me and that I needed to forgive as well. This was a process that didn't happen suddenly in a bolt of forgiveness. I may never see this coach again on earth, but if I do, I can honestly say that I have reached the place where I can say I forgive him, wish him well and want him as my friend.

I want to make a bold statement here. *The concept of forgiveness is one of the most misunderstood of all the Christian doctrines.*

I struggled most of my life with the pain of hurts, trying to come to resolution with the truth of the Bible. It's not easy to forget the pain of abuse. And yet scripture said I needed to submit that desire for revenge to God for healing. Hate has a way of permeating our very being and rearing its ugly head at the most inopportune times. It can wreak havoc with relationships and affect the way we minister to others even when we try to hide it. We can pretend we are at peace while the fury rages within, just under the surface.

Published in the May, 2004 *Reader's Digest* is a powerful article that addresses the power of forgiveness.

"THE POWER OF FORGIVENESS, THE BEST WAY TO HEAL A HEART"
BY LISA COLLIER COOL

Elizabeth Nassau was stunned. She had called a good friend to wish her a happy birthday, when suddenly she found herself under attack. "Out of the blue, she launched a long list of everything that bothered her about me, and dumped me over the phone," says the 48 year-old writer from Philadelphia.

Nassau blames jealousy: "My career was just starting to get off the ground. My book was about to be published, and I'd won an award for my essays. I felt my friend didn't like it that I wasn't needy anymore."

She spent two years fuming. "Every time I saw her, my blood boiled, my heart pounded and I'd get so tense that I literally felt sick."

Who hasn't felt the sting of betrayal, unfair treatment or something more abusive? Many of us cling to the resulting rage and pain, but others choose not to. The latest research shows that learning to forgive those who hurt us can have profound benefits. It's become a hot new way to manage anger, cut stress and, maybe most important, improve health. At an Atlanta conference last fall, some 40 researchers met to review what they're finding in probing the healing power of making peace. One study showed that giving up grudges can reduce chronic back pain. Another found that forgiveness limited relapses among women battling substance abuse problems. One intriguing project discussed at the event—run by the nonprofit Campaign for Forgiveness Research—used MRI scans to explore how just thinking about empathy and reconciliation sparks activity in the brain's left middle temporal gyrus, suggesting we all have a mental forgiveness center set to be tapped.

So on top of having profound emotional benefits, purging our anger may also help heal some of what ails us physically. But how do we do it? And what does it mean to forgive?

NO STRINGS ATTACHED

Elizabeth Nassau's revelation came at a chance meeting with her estranged friend: "Instead of turning away, I told her how profoundly she had hurt me. She listened, but didn't apologize. Then I surprised myself. I apologized for harboring anger and hatred against her for so long. As I spoke, I realized I'd forgiven her."

The effect was potent. "My anger melted away," she says. Nassau hasn't renewed the friendship, but now when she sees her ex-pal, "I can breathe calmly and my heart isn't palpitating."

Nassau's experience fits with the findings of Fred Luskin, PhD, director at Stanford University's Forgiveness project and author of *Forgive for Good*. Luskin—quick to emphasize that forgiveness doesn't mean condoning the offence—has found that letting go of a grudge can slash one's stress level by up to 50 percent. Volunteers in his studies also have shown improvements in energy, mood, sleep quality and overall physical vitality. "Carrying around a load of bitterness and anger at how unfairly you were treated is very toxic," says Luskin.

That's because we're wired to treat any tension-inducing event, be it a fire alarm or relieving a simmering feud, as crisis. At these times, our bodies release the stress hormones adrenaline and cortisol, prompting our hearts to accelerate, our breath to quicken and our minds to race. An accompanying sugar release revs up muscles, and clotting factors surge in the blood. It's all harmless if the scare is brief (like a near mishap on the highway). But anger and resentment are like accidents that don't end, turning hormones meant to save us into toxins.

Cortisol's depressive effect on the immune system has been linked to serious disorders. Bruce McEwen, PhD, director of the neuroendocrinology lab at Rockefeller University in New York City, says cortisol wears down the brain, leading to cell atrophy and memory loss. It also raises the blood pressure and blood sugar, hardening of the arteries and leading to heart disease.

Enter forgiveness, which seems to stop these hormones from flowing. For a study presented to the American Psychosomatic Society last March, University of Michigan-Madison researchers recruited 36 male veterans who had coronary artery disease and were also burdened by painful issues, some was-related, some tied to marital problems. Work conflicts or childhood traumas. Half the men received forgiveness training; the rest didn't. Those who got the training showed greater blood flow to the heart.

Just thinking about resolving a hurt can help. In a 2001 study, psychologist Charlotte vanOyen Witvliet, PhD, of Hope College in Holland, Michigan, hooked 71 college students to sensors and had them relive lies, insults or betrayals by family members, friends or lovers. Told to imagine forgiving the offenders, the subjects experienced heart rates and blood pressure two and a half times lower than when they thought about holding a grudge. "It appears that forgiveness could be a powerful antidote to anger, which is strongly associated with chronically elevated blood pressure and increased risk for heart disease," says Witvliet.

That makes sense to Sandra Lamb. After growing worried last year about her 82-year-old father's poor driving, the Denver woman confronted him.

"I told him he really should consider not driving anymore, because it was getting dangerous," Lamb says. "He got so angry he was shaking, and said, 'I've been driving all my life—and no one is going to take my car keys.' Then he told me he never wanted to see me again." Lamb was so upset and angry that she was unable to to talk to her father for seven months. Eventually, though, she felt she had to reconcile with him before it was too late. She went to visit him. "I told my father I was sorry about how I handled the driving issue, and apologized for upsetting him." And she forgave him for lashing out. "He hugged me and said, 'That's okay.' I was very happy and thankful to have our relationship restored.." Health problems soon made the driving dispute moot.

Take it as it is

Despite its benefits, many of us won't even consider forgiveness an option. That, Witvliet says, is a big mistake: "Hanging on to resentment for months or years means making a commitment to remain angry."

Take Catherine O'Brien. After her 1992 divorce, the Pacifica, California, video producer spent years hating her ex-husband. She was angry about how the split ruined her future.

"Suddenly, I was a single parent with a 12-year-old daughter. It was exhausting and disappointing not to have someone to share the carpools, the doctors' visits and the joy of having a child, when I thought we'd raise a family together."

The anger took its toll. "I was tense and uptight all the time, constantly got colds, and was always tired," says O'Brien, 55.

Even more upsetting was how other people saw her. "At a party, someone introduced me to a woman, saying, 'Her husband left her too.' I was shocked that I'd become identified as an embittered ex-wife."

Then she heard an audiotape of Fred Luskin speaking, "It was like a light bulb going on: I realized the only person I was hurting was myself." She told her ex-husband she was moving on and felt profound relief. "A weight was lifted off my shoulders, and I started feeling much healthier."

Luskin says resolving such resentment "releases hostile feelings with positive ones that make your body feel calm and relaxed, which enhances health." In one of his studies, seventeen adults from Northern Ireland who lost a relative to terrorist violence got a week of forgiveness training. Their mental distress dropped by 40 percent, and they saw a 35 percent dip in headaches, back pain and insomnia.

O'Brien and others may balk at forgiveness because they misunderstand what it is, explains Luskin. "It in no way means the offence was okay, or that you should let yourself be treated unfairly.". . .

Luskin says resolving such resentment "replaces hostile feelings with positive ones that make your body feel calm and relaxed, which enhances health." In one of his studies, seventeen adults from Northern Ireland who lost a relative to terrorist violence got a week of forgiveness training. Their mental distress dropped by forty percent, and they saw a thirty-five percent dip in headaches, back pain and insomnia.

O'Brien and others may balk at forgiveness because they misunderstand what it is, explains Luskin. "It in no way means the offence was okay, or that you should let yourself be treated unfairly.". . .

However you defuse your anger, forgiveness can be powerful. And while you can't alter the past, confronting unresolved issues and the people behind them can lead you to a happier, healthier future."

Remember the four steps through forgiveness? Hurt, hate, healing and happiness. They will not necessarily happen in order.

Unforgiveness is like a cancer cell that demands it own way. Normal cells divide and become new cells. The cancer cell, on the other hand, stops dividing and gathers other cells to it, growing out of control.

Love is like the normal cell that divides and produces new healthy cells. Hate, on the other hand, gathers other cells to it, and grows uncontrollable, spreading and wreaking havoc in our lives.

CHAPTER TWENTY EIGHT

Let the Healing Begin

When you forgive someone for hurting you, you perform spiritual surgery inside your very soul. You cut away the festering injured flesh, and allow the Spirit to help you see the injuring party as God sees him. In my case, I had to reprogram my mind to see the coach as God sees him. Some of the blame for the incident was mine, since I had an attitude problem to begin with. For his part, I have to concede that the coach was new at teaching, new to my school, new to the area, and unfamiliar with the students. He had a huge task ahead of him. I will venture to say he was probably very frightened of failing at his task, and probably had no idea how to handle a hearing impaired and difficult student. In the end, I had to believe that he did the best he knew with the tools at hand. When I saw him in this light and asked God to help me love him, my attitude began to change from hatred to understanding. Though I'll never forget what he did, I can now see him as a lost sheep whom God loves and is seeking.

When forgiveness illuminates the truth about the person who hurt us, we can suddenly identify with their humanness and the reasons for their behavior. We are suddenly able to understand and to get past the hatred.

Forgiveness produces a new understanding and a transformed attitude in the person who chooses to forgive. Because this is such an important point, let me say it again. *Forgiveness produces a new understanding and a transformed attitude in the person who chooses to forgive.*

If I had not chosen to forgive the coach, I would still, to this day be enslaved by my past hurts. I reversed the course of my future by releasing him from hate and resentment. Forgiveness is even effective when the person responsible is no longer in the picture.

The first stage of healing from unforgiveness is that of release. After relinquishing our right to hold a grudge, we gain the ability to wish the person no harm. Shortly, we will even wish that person well.

The stages of forgiveness were made clear to me as I pondered Corrie ten Boom's triumphant illustration of forgiveness. If you recall, Corrie ten Boom was a Dutch gentile who lived with her father and sister when Hitler's troops began to invade Holland. With orders to round up and deport to concentration camps all Jewish citizens, even the mention of Hitler's name brought fear and trembling to all who heard it.

Because of their faith in Christ, this family chose to obey God's urging to protect those He loved, so they began to hide Jews in their home. After a time, the Germans learned of the plan, and arrested the family, hauling them off to those same concentration camps.

Both Corrie's father and sister died in the interment camps, leaving her alone to share about goodness of God in times of trial.

After a service where she had preached on forgiveness, a man approached her, admitting he was one who was responsible for exterminating Jews in concentration camps.

The man asked, "God has forgiven me. Can you do the same?"

Corrie readily admits to being consumed by hatred at that moment.

She prayed, "God, I can't forgive him. I hate him. Please, help me."

The man had his hand extended to shake, and though her first impulse was to hit him, she chose to shake his hand. In choosing to forgive him, she felt a wonderful release of the hatred, and even felt a deep sense of peace. Forgiveness doesn't negate the truth of the hurt you endured. It simply disarms that wound from causing you further pain.

I met a woman who struggled with shortness of breath. She spent untold amounts of money on doctors, medications, breathing treatments and oxygen. She dreaded lying down to sleep because she could not breathe and worried that she would die in the night.

Some time later, her sister became ill and seemed on the verge of death. The woman, who had never been close to her sister, went to see her and the two reconciled just before the sister died.

From that time on, the woman's breathing problems improved, until finally she had no need for treatment at all. The underlying cause was clearly unforgiveness. The sister had stolen this woman's boyfriend many years earlier, leaving her feeling betrayed and wounded.

When she finally chose to forgive her sister, her body began to function normally.

Expect hurts to come into your life. Recognize the hurt for what it is, seeing the one who hurt you as a work in progress. Remember that hurting people hurt other people. Release the hate and hurt to God and allow Him to put salve on the wound. Isaiah 61:6 (KJV) says, "*He hath sent me to bind up the brokenhearted.*"

The original word for bind up is chavash, meaning, "to bind a wrap around, bind up as a wound, bandage, cover, envelope, enclose." Strong adds a very visual definition to the same word. "To compress...to stop."

Scripture defines a broken heart as one that is hemorrhaging. In this case, to bind is akin to applying pressure to a badly bleeding wound.

What a wonderful picture of Christ! A crushing hurt shatters us, and the sympathetic, scarred hand of Christ presses on the wound, and just for a moment, the pain seems to intensify. But finally the bleeding stops so the wound can begin to heal.

Are you able to envision the tender involvement of Christ when you're devastated? And to think this is the same One we accuse of not caring when that crushing moment occurs.

Notice that the first definition of binding up includes covering, enveloping and enclosing. Have you ever noticed that when your heart is broken, you tend to feel exposed and less in control of your emotions? Truly, few situations cause us to be more vulnerable than at such emotionally fragile moments. After being hurt repeatedly, it is natural for us to want to raise a thick tower around ourselves, vowing never to be hurt again. And though that's a normal human response, it is not God's way. Those same fortresses erected to protect us also keep love and healing from reaching us. Only God can put the pieces of a broken heart together again, closing up all the wounds and wrapping it in a bandage that will protect from infection, yet still let healing oxygen flood the wound.

Are you in bondage to a broken heart you have never let Christ bind up and heal? Right now, you can, for the very first time, give Him access to your wound. When you choose to lower your guard and let Him tenderly minister to your need, beloved, you will truly never be the same again.

Epilogue

When we come to Jesus Christ as Savior from our sins we are made in right relationship with a holy God. We are to have life and have it more abundantly. Because I was wounded I chose to go away from the fellowship of this relationship. The year 2001 is when this prodigal son came humbly back to his Father. I had a friend, teacher, mentor, who helped me put my testimony into print. I would like to share my coming back to Jesus Christ with you. I call this my *"Hidden Village Experience"* because it happened at the Hidden Village apartments in Bethlehem, PA.

FROM COMA TO WRITER IN A SECOND

The young boy leaned back from the bridge rail, bracing for the throw. Every muscle in his skinny ten year old frame tensed as he wound up, and then hurled the rock into the pool. Rushing to the rail's edge, he smiled as ripple after ripple unfurled its way from the place where the stone entered the water. Although the rock sunk into the water's depth, the ripples it made persisted on their path, one after the other, seeming never to end. The boy had no idea how serious those ripples could be.

I, like that rock, sank into a pool of despair after a traumatic divorce separated me not only from my wife, but from my son, my foster son, and my career. The ripples I created by these difficult days sent hurt far beyond the immediate impact. Although I lay alive at the bottom of the pool

137

of troubles, I might as well have been dead. It was as if I was in a coma. My body functions continued, but my spiritual life was unproductive and dead.

Time has a way of healing the body or even a wounded spirit, but when you are in a spiritual coma there is only one way to come out of it. The way out is through a supernatural healing of the Holy Spirit.

Can a man describe lightning? It comes across the sky in a streak and then it is gone. But it lights up its surroundings and is gone in the twinkling of an eye. The Father God, through the Holy Spirit, lifted me up to a higher plain. My heart was racing in my chest so hard I could feel it in my throat because I was standing on holy ground, the light so bright, and the Presence so real that I heard in my innermost being, "Jesus loves you. He died for you. Get back into a right relationship with Him."

In that light, all I could see was how sinful I was and I cried out, "I'm no good. I'm just a piece of junk."

The gentle precious breath whispered so lovingly, "I Am made you, you're my child. I didn't create junk."

I could not contain my emotions any longer, and I began to weep. As I sat there in that state of euphoria weeping and praising God, this heavenly visitor continued to converse with me and asked with all the authority of heaven, "What do you want?" In this state of grace thoughts were conceptual, and I, knowing full well all that was involved and the impact of the written word, answered in complete confidence, "Lord, I want to write about you."

Then one word, "*Journal.*"

Now that I was alive to the spiritual things again, I was able to tune into the Holy Spirit's prompting. He gave me an insatiable appetite to read God's Word and pray. He made the Word come alive.

I was obedient and did start to journal. He taught me how to write and pray. He impressed on my heart to write my prayers in a composition book. I am ashamed to say this, but in my entire Christian walk, prayer was one of my weakest areas. In just a short period of time He helped me to pray two hours a day and stay focused. Hallelujah! What a Savior!

The Holy Spirit gave me a song in my heart and helped me write this poem:

I used to say:
Only one life, will soon be past
Only what's done for Christ will last.

Now I say:
Only one life has so soon passed by,
Only what should have been done for Christ
Makes me know how time does fly.
It's almost over now,
And before the Mercy Seat I'll bow
I'll ask forgiveness for the loss of time,
And a seat at the foot of the table will be mine.

Endnotes

1. Graham, Billy, *Hope for the Troubled Heart,* copyright 1991 by Word Books, Irving Texas Pp. 114-115.
2. ibid. P.115.
3. Wilkerson, David, *Have You Felt Like Ivimg Up Lately?* Copyright 1980 by Garden Valley Publishers
   Published by Fleming H. Revell
   A division of Baker book House Co.
   P.O.Box 6287, Grand Rapids, Michigan 49516-6287 Pp. 47-48.
4. ibid P. 19.
5. MacDonald, Gordon, *Rebuilding Your Broken World,* Copyright 1988, 1990 Thomas Nelson Publishers, Nashville, Tennessee, Pp22,23,25. Used by permission. All rights reserved.
6. Thomas, Major Ian, *The Saving Life of Christ,* Copyright 1961, Zondervan, Grand Rapids, Michigan, Pp. 35-36.
7. MacDonald, ibid. Pp 42-43.
8. Tada, Joni Erickson, Estes, Steven, *When God Weeps,* Zondervan Publishing House, Grand Rapids, Michigan, 1997, Pp 53-54.
9. Thomas, Ibid. Pp. 35-36.
10. Thomas, ibid 14-15.

Printed in the United States
91573LV00001B/37-135/A